CHINESE INVESTMENT AND INFLUENCE IN EUROPE

HEARING

BEFORE THE

SUBCOMMITTEE ON EUROPE, EURASIA, AND EMERGING THREATS

OF THE

COMMITTEE ON FOREIGN AFFAIRS
HOUSE OF REPRESENTATIVES

ONE HUNDRED FIFTEENTH CONGRESS

SECOND SESSION

MAY 23, 2018

Serial No. 115–134

Printed for the use of the Committee on Foreign Affairs

Available: http://www.foreignaffairs.house.gov/, http://docs.house.gov, or http://www.gpo.gov/fdsys/

U.S. GOVERNMENT PUBLISHING OFFICE

30–178PDF　　　　WASHINGTON : 2018

CONTENTS

Page

WITNESSES

Mr. Philippe Le Corre, senior fellow, Mossavar-Rahmani Center for Business and Government, John F. Kennedy School of Government, Harvard University 5
Mr. Gordon Chang, author 17
Mr. Kevin D. Freeman, author 29

LETTERS, STATEMENTS, ETC., SUBMITTED FOR THE HEARING

Mr. Philippe Le Corre: Prepared statement 8
Mr. Gordon Chang: Prepared statement 19
Mr. Kevin D. Freeman: Prepared statement 32

APPENDIX

Hearing notice 54
Hearing minutes 55

CHINESE INVESTMENT AND INFLUENCE IN EUROPE

WEDNESDAY, MAY 23, 2018

House of Representatives,
Subcommittee on Europe, Eurasia, and Emerging Threats,
Committee on Foreign Affairs,
Washington, DC.

The subcommittee met, pursuant to notice, at 2 o'clock p.m., in room 2255 Rayburn House Office Building, Hon. Dana Rohrabacher (chairman of the subcommittee) presiding.

Mr. ROHRABACHER. This hearing is called to order.

In nearly two decades—it's been nearly two decades—since China entered the World Trade Organization in 2001, and since then America has experienced a debilitating consequence of unfair trade, and that is unfair trade with the People's Republic of China.

And it has been a relationship since that time that has sometimes been dubbed as an economic blood transfusion from West to East—a vast transfer of wealth that has financed the Chinese security state at home and a coercive military foreign policy abroad.

Yet, America has not been the only target. China, likewise, seeks economic and political advantage over Europe and that is the subject of today's hearing.

According to an open source data, which is likely to underestimate such true figures, direct investment from China into Europe now stands at $95 billion a year and China has bought or invested well over $300 billion in European assets in the last decade. That is a significant sum. But those figures do not do justice to the scale and breadth of influence that China has thus achieved.

Chinese investment, much of it directed by the state-owned enterprises of China, reflects and serves the political goals of Beijing.

China is a global strategy—it has a global strategy—to control the extraction of raw resources, to control transportation corridors, to dominate the innovation and production cycles of others, and then to sell the products it has abroad to enrich the corrupt elite that rule over China today.

As has been much discussed elsewhere, the Belt and Road Initiative is part of this grand strategy as are Chinese efforts to set up a stage—an event for letting them do Arctic shipping between Europe and Asia as well as, of course, the creation of a parallel regional platform such as 16+1.

For China, Europe represents a large market with few economic defenses like we have in the United States. So Europe is relatively vulnerable compared to our country to this type of economic challenge.

For example, while the Committee on Foreign Investment in the United States—better known as CFIUS—has blunted some of China's attempts to buy key companies in the United States, only 12 of the 28 European Union member states have a comparable mechanism to screen for an investment and also screen the efforts to create and an EU-wide system has proven unsuccessful. So they don't have it now and it doesn't look like it's in the works. I am interested in hearing what our witnesses will say about that.

Likewise, Chinese political influence operations have found opportunities in Europe. There are now over 440 Confucius Institutes and classrooms in Europe, often partnering with credentialed local educational institutes.

These Confucius Institutes are, ultimately, and they are ultimately the spokesman for the Chinese Communist Party and the transition belts that inject Chinese propaganda directly into the education of European youth.

Despite the differences between the United States and Europe, we broadly share a commitment to human rights and rule of law. China is using economic leverage to weaken and divide the West.

Economically, China seeks to prevent either American or European companies from competing against Chinese companies abroad, especially in the Indo-Pacific and also areas and politically they have been involved in the transatlantic community trying to speak about this—about this threat has been thwarted by the Chinese themselves within Europe and within the United States.

So we can't even now talk about, and I've noticed this in the film business—this is in my notes here—I've noticed in the film business, the Chinese have invested in the film business in the United States and all of a sudden you see positive Chinese characters emerging in films that have nothing to do about China.

Well, this type of influence that they've been using has prevented the type of criticism that China deserves about the destruction of Tibet, East Turkestan, the murder of Falun Gong prisoners, the plight of political dissidents, the elimination of the political opposition in Hong Kong, the suppression and infiltration of Christian churches in China, and, of course, the issue of the sovereignty of Taiwan.

These issues have not been able to be discussed or at least the discussion of these issues are undermined by Beijing's efforts economically as well as politically.

So Beijing seeks to use its influence to create scenarios where the Western governments and private companies are preemptively obedient and kowtow to the interests of China because they have laid the groundwork intellectually for undermining these charges against them.

In this contest for influence and dominance, the United States and Europe—we have no choice but to work together. I say to my European colleagues that protection is not protectionism.

So we must all agree that not all investment is equal. Financing from Brussels or New York is fundamentally different than money that is offered by China.

And perhaps the terms could be cheaper than what the Chinese offer or the credit could free—be a freer flowing. But I can promise anyone who takes part of this, you will be paying more in the end by taking such deals.

With that, I would like to yield to my ranking member, Mr. Meeks, for his opening statement and then I will ask our witnesses to proceed with 5-minute statements and then we will have a dialogue.

So with that said, Mr. Meeks.

Mr. MEEKS. Good afternoon, everyone, and thank you for being here. Thank you, Chairman Rohrabacher, for calling our attention to the ongoing concern of ours that affects both sides of the Atlantic—Chinese direct investment and the associated strategic implications.

Large investments from China are not necessarily new. But as China's foreign policy adapts and sharpens into one of economic diplomacy, we should be aware of their goals and their intentions, overt or covert.

Moreover, is it important to understand where the money is going and to determine just how strategic these sectors are. This is especially significant, given the monolithic nature of the Chinese Government and the fact that the majority of the foreign direct investment in the EU from China are led by state-owned enterprises.

Europe, including countries beyond the EU, is an enormous market and our largest trading partner. The targets of Chinese investment in this market has evolved over the last decade or so.

Although Central Europe is becoming a more attractive and welcoming place for Chinese investment, notably, in the 16+1 framework, the vast majority is going to Western Europe.

Incidentally, it is the Western European countries that push forward a European approach to the strategic nature of these investments.

These type of investments are also important to examine from infrastructure, technology, to lax residency programs. The interest is clear.

As a senior member of the House Financial Services Committee, I am specifically interested in how we screen investments into the United States.

And here on the Subcommittee of Europe, I am searching for ways to cooperate with our European allies to keep our financial bodies robust, healthy, and free of nefarious influence.

Our open markets are sometimes used as an entry port for nefarious activity or simply to hide ill-gained money.

As a first step, I would like to see a degree of more transparency in ownership rules so that, at minimum, we could know more about who is investing in what.

It is this sense this hearing can be all about state-directed financing into our systems including those directed by the Kremlin, for example.

And why should we care about these types of investments? First off, the investments are not purely commercial. There are strings attached.

Secondly, although we can and should cooperate with China on common areas of concern, such as North Korea, it is a competitor that does not share our common values—democracy and respect for individual rights.

Hopes that China was moving in a democratic future have been dashed, leading some here in the United States and many in Europe with a more realistic vision of today's China.

Thirdly, China has not been reciprocal in market access and there's an element of fairness that should be addressed in international fora, not solely on Twitter.

Regardless, in all of the aforementioned areas, I am keen on seeing on how we can avoid widening the current rift in the transatlantic relations, avoid unnecessary trade spats, all important, and let us work together earnestly with our European allies to protect the transatlantic project and the values we live by.

I believe cooperation with the EU on this topic can bring us a closer—can bring us closer. In fact, I encourage the Trump administration to approach it this way.

Let's not shoot ourselves in the foot by alienating our closest allies and partners. Doing so only plays into the hands of Moscow and Beijing.

So I look forward to hearing from our panel about how we should address this issue. It should be of transatlantic concern to all of us.

I yield back.

Mr. ROHRABACHER. Mr. Cicilline, would you like to have a short opening statement?

Mr. CICILLINE. Thank you, Chairman Rohrabacher and Ranking Member Meeks, for convening today's hearing to discuss Chinese investment, influence in Europe, and thank you for our witnesses for being here.

China has shown time and again that it is more than happy to fill a void whenever we recede, and I just want to use my minute to talk about one very specific example, something I've been a lot of time working on but I think which really illustrates the challenge, and that is the use of a former U.S. Air Force Base at Lajes located on the Azorian Islands in Portugal.

The U.S. and Portugal have had a long and rich history and partnership together since World War II and until recently Lajes was a key installation linking the U.S. to Europe and the Middle East.

It boasts the largest runway in Europe, capable of supporting any commercial or military aircraft in the U.S. or NATO fleet.

It was used during the Cold War and is a crucial stepping stone in operations ranging from the Berlin airlift to the Gulf War.

However, in 2016, the Department of Defense decided to decommission Lajes, a decision I strongly opposed for a lot of reasons, but not the least of which was it became clear that by vacating that space it would open up a strategic position to outside influences.

In the past year, China has shown interest in investing in Lajes, and the Azores may be left in the position where they have to welcome them in order for this area to survive.

This would lead to a previously unthinkable circumstance—the Government of China with a perch in the North Atlantic between the United States and Europe.

This is just one example of Chinese interests in Europe, which I believe the U.S. needs to take very seriously. I look forward to the hearing from our witnesses today and thank you, again, Mr. Chairman, for convening this hearing.

Mr. ROHRABACHER. Thank you very much for your opening statement.

I remember when I first found out that the Chinese had bought these terminals on both ends of the Panama Canal—how concerned I was and what you have raised should be also of equal concern to us. Thank you very much for that opening statement.

And now we will go to our witnesses, and again, I would like if we could have 5 minutes for opening testimony, then a discussion. That's what this—these hearings are all about.

And our first witness is Philippe Le Corre—Le Corre—is that pronounced correctly?

Mr. LE CORRE. Le Corre.

Mr. ROHRABACHER. Le Corre. All right. And he is a senior fellow with the Carnegie Endowment for International Peace and senior fellow at the Harvard's Kennedy School of Government. He has worked in several positions—senior positions in the French Ministry of Defense and has been focused on Asia and that responsibility. His latest books is "China's Offensive in Europe," published in 2016.

You may proceed.

STATEMENT OF MR. PHILIPPE LE CORRE, SENIOR FELLOW, MOSSAVAR-RAHMANI CENTER FOR BUSINESS AND GOVERNMENT, JOHN F. KENNEDY SCHOOL OF GOVERNMENT, HARVARD UNIVERSITY

Mr. LE CORRE. Thank you, Mr. Chairman.

Chairman Rohrabacher, Ranking Member Meeks, distinguished members of this committee, it's an honor for me to testify and hearing on this subject by other subcommittees in this very House I am delighted that your subcommittee has decided to address this important topic.

I've been working on Chinese investments in Europe for several years and I've brought actually my book—the one you mentioned, Chairman—and it has indeed become quite a topic over the past 2 years.

And it's not just a topic for Europeans. It is also relevant, as you mentioned, to the United States, which count many European nations as its friends and partners.

Last month's state visit by President Macron in this Congress was clear evidence of this friendship.

The current national security strategy of the United States stresses, "China's strategic foothold in Europe where it is extending its unfair trade practices and investing in key industries, sensitive technologies, and infrastructure."

It also calls for dialogue with European allies "to contest China's unfair trade and economic practices and restricts its acquisition of sensitive technologies."

What I will try to do in the next few minutes is to describe some of the current trends of China's overseas foreign direct investments in the European Union and beyond.

First, Chinese projects are on the rise. From $840 million invested in 2008 they grew to $42 billion in 2017. According to a recent compilation by Bloomberg, total Chinese investments in Europe, including both mergers and acquisitions and greenfield investments, amount to $318 billion.

Second, these investments cover many sectors, consumer brands, services, industry, high technologies, and infrastructure.

Third, they are spread out across the continent. The United Kingdom comes first as China is trying to build in the city of London its first international RMB platform.

Germany, which is the EU's largest and best performing economy, comes next, followed by Italy, France, Finland, Portugal, Greece, and Poland.

Depending on the size of the economy and the type of targets, you will find a nuclear plant construction in England, a robotics company partly financed by China in Germany, or an automobile brand in Sweden. In the vast majority of cases, Chinese investments have been initiated and operated by state-owned companies.

There are, indeed, some private investors—about a third—but in most cases they have received funding from state banks or Chinese sovereign funds.

In particular, I would like to point out the cases of Portugal and Greece, two relatively small economies which have thrown open the gates to Chinese investors.

In the Portuguese case, the 2008 financial crisis led the government to privatize a number of utilities including Energias de Portugal (EDP), the largest electricity operator. The Chinese company, China Three Gorges, is now offering to take over the entire EDP.

One can easily imagine the national security risk if this EU and NATO country was to sell its national grid to a foreign power.

In the Greek case, again, the financial crisis in Europe has led the government to privatize the Piraeus Harbor. The Chinese state-owned company Cosco now runs 67 percent of the harbor.

China is using Piraeus as its main hub in the Mediterranean region with the clear goal of expanding its exports to Europe through the maritime rules.

One question that experts have been wondering about is whether Chinese FDI should all be considered part of the so-called Silk Road investments. As often in the case of China, the response is opportunistic.

Those that are part of the Belt and Road Initiative and controlled by the state can be integrated in that scheme. But others, because they don't feed the plan or because their home countries have not signed into the BRI are not.

Launched in 2013, the BRI's network of infrastructure projects including railways, roads, ports, airports, telecommunication links, oil and gas pipelines, and energy facilities, today the BRI is the centerpiece of China's foreign and domestic policies.

But it is not solely aimed at Europe. It is now a broad concept, even a global geoeconomic strategy. The fact that Chinese entities partially or wholly own at least four airports and six seaports is no coincidence—even if some of these deals were signed before the BRI, they are now a part of the plan which includes developing massively e-commerce across Europe, which require huge logistical capacities.

China so far failed to get a substantial number of European countries interested in the BRI. Polls show a lack of knowledge about the initiative in most European countries.

The leaders of Germany, France, the U.K., all skipped the Belt and Road forum in Beijing in May 2017 as did the president of the European Commission.

Instead, the latter sent one of his vice presidents, who said that any scheme connecting Europe and Asia should adhere to a number of principles, including market rules and international procurement standards and should complement existing networks and policies.

It is fair to say that the BRI presents opportunities for Europe. But it is primarily a Chinese project that will help China expand its influence in the Eurasian region and beyond.

Europe and China have similar aims in their respective territories, preserving jobs, fueling economy growth, and maintaining social stability.

However, they have a different way of pursuing these goals and may achieve them better by staying somewhat apart, which is why, Mr. Chairman, I have been advocating in my writings that Europe should speak to like-minded nations and territories to analyze and assess the rise of Chinese investment and of the Silk Road project, keeping in mind the need for transparency, reciprocity, and respect of the rule-based international order.

Tomorrow, Chancellor Angela Merkel will travel to Beijing and she'll be able to, hopefully, stand, not only for her country's interests but also those international rules.

Next month, when leaders of the G-7 meet in Canada, I also think it should be part of the private conversations among leaders to address this issue of China's investments.

Thank you.

[The prepared statement of Mr. Le Corre follows:]

**Testimony before the House of Representatives Foreign Affairs Committee
Subcommittee on Europe, Eurasia and Emerging Threats**

Hearing on Chinese Investment and Influence in Europe

- May 23, 2018 -

**Philippe Le Corre
Carnegie Endowment for International Peace & Harvard Kennedy School**

Chairman Rohrabacher, Ranking Member Meeks, distinguished members of this committee, thank you for inviting me to testify.

The topic that we are addressing today has become increasingly relevant not just to European countries but also – as described in the latest and current National Security Strategy – to the United States[1]. For the first time, the NSS underlines China's "strategic foothold" in Europe, "where it is expanding its unfair trade practices and investing in key industries, sensitive technologies and infrastructure." China's overseas investments are no longer of concern to individual countries. For example, just two weeks ago, the company China Three Gorges offered $11 billion to take over the entire capital of *Energias de Portugal*-EDP, Portugal's largest grid company, with subsidiaries in the United States, Spain and Brazil. The Portuguese government says that the markets should decide, but what would happen if the largest electricity company of a member of the European Union (EU) and the North Atlantic Treaty Organization (NATO) were to be handed to a foreign country? What would it mean for the sovereignty or national security of Portugal, and for the organizations to which it belongs?

In the time available, I will address the following points:
1/ The landscape of Chinese foreign investments in Europe: a quick overview
2/ Ties between "traditional" Foreign Direct Investments (FDI) and "Silk Road" investments
3/ The ongoing debate in the European Parliament over screening Chinese foreign investments

1/ The landscape of Chinese FDI in Europe

Since 2008, the landscape of Chinese foreign direct investments in the European Union has changed dramatically.

---

[1] The views presented here are those of the author, and do not represent those of the Carnegie Endowment for International Peace or the Harvard Kennedy School

Two years ago, I published a book on the subject, *China's Offensive in Europe*[2], describing China's wave of post-2008 financial crisis investments. Since then, numbers have reached new heights, and projects have spread across the continent.

From $840 million invested in 2008, China's annual FDI in Europe grew to $42 billion in 2017. According to a recent compilation by Bloomberg[3], total Chinese investments in Europe, including both mergers and acquisitions (M&A) and greenfield investments, amount to $318 billion, 45 percent more than Chinese investment in the U.S. between 2008 and 2017. China has taken over approximately 360 European companies.

Although last year saw a slight decline, it is fair to say that the long-term trend of China investing in European brands, technology and infrastructures will continue. China's investments are also broadly spread geographically, although the largest European economies – the United Kingdom ($70 billion in cumulative Chinese investment), Italy ($31 billion), Germany ($20 billion), and France ($13 billion) – attract the largest share of Chinese capital. Among China's iconic investments in Europe is the Hinkley Point nuclear plant in southern England, which is one third funded by China.

For over a decade now, the City of London has been a magnet for Chinese cash as Beijing tries to build its currency, the RMB, into a world currency. By and large, Chinese money has been going into real estate and finance, with Chinese state banks well represented and active in the bond market and the international exchange market. Chinese citizens represent almost half of the investor visas the UK granted in 2017, outnumbering Russians, the next largest group of investor visa recipients, by 250 percent[4]. Despite the largely uncertain future of the UK as a market once it exits the EU, China is betting on the British capital as an emerging hub of Chinese finance.

In Germany, China's investments started with the purchase of family-run industrial companies, such as machine-tool maker *Putzmeister* in 2010, and continued with the Chinese company *Midea's* acquisition of robotics company *Kuka AG* in 2016 for $5.2 billion. More recently, a Chinese investor's $1 billion acquisition made it became the top shareholder of Daimler AG. German debate over Chinese FDI has intensified since the launch in 2015 of China's *Made in China 2025* strategy, a national plan that aims to make the country a champion in key high-tech industries such as aerospace, robotics, and artificial intelligence. Many Chinese companies have eyed German companies with the goal of acquiring technologies and orchestrating transfers of these technologies.

In Italy, China's Silk Road Fund helped *China National Chemical Corporation,* also known as *ChemChina,* buy tire maker *Pirelli* in 2015 for $7.7billion. *ChemChina* has also acquired a string of industrial and energy related companies.

---

[2] *China's Offensive in Europe*, Washington, D.C.: Brookings Institution Press, 2016

[3] https://www.bloomberg.com/graphics/2018-china-business-in-europe/

[4] https://www.ft.com/content/d91bac2c-3752-11e8-8eee-e06bde01c544

In the EU's immediate neighbourhood, Switzerland has captured the lion's share of Chinese FDI with *ChemChina's* acquisition of *Syngenta*, one of the world's largest agri-business conglomerates. The deal was finalized in 2018 for $46 billion, making it the world's single largest acquisition by a Chinese company.

The islands of Cyprus and Malta, both full EU member-states, are throwing open the gates to Chinese investors, especially in finance and real estate. Both have also become strong supporters of China. Then there are the cases of Greece and Portugal, two Southern European countries that together account for a modest 2.5 percent of the EU's GDP in 2017.

China has become a key-investor in Greece, mainly through a central investment project. In 2016, a Chinese state-owned corporation, *China Ocean Shipping Company (Cosco)*, took over 67 per cent of Athens' Piraeus harbour. China has signalled that it intends to use this port as the main platform for its maritime Silk Road, part of Beijing's "Belt and Road" Initiative. Most Chinese companies are now using Piraeus as their principal port of entry in Southern Europe. Visiting China in 2016, Prime Minister Alexis Tsipras declared that Greece intends to "serve as China's gateway into Europe".

To the west, Portugal has become a key recipient of Chinese investment. Per capita, it is one of the largest in Europe. During a Euro region's crisis in 2011, the Lisbon government was under pressure from the European Commission, the European Central Bank, and the International Monetary Fund (IMF), the so-called "troika," to sell state assets. China stepped forward to offer foreign investment. As part of the bailout, China Three Gorges bought 26 per cent of EDP, and State Grid Corp. of China bought a stake in Portugal's power distributor, *REN-Redes Energeticas Nacionais SA*. *Fosun* Group, a privately-owned Shanghai-based company, controls the Portugal's largest insurer, *Fidelidade,* and a group of private hospitals, just to mention a few of the more prominent deals.

State-owned enterprises from China have initiated more than two thirds of Chinese investments across the European continent. Chinese sovereign funds or state banks have financed other deals by private investors, illustrating Beijing's use of state-directed, market-distorting, mercantilist policies. A truly market-based economy remains a distant prospect for today's China.

Chinese investments cover a wide-range of sectors that can be divided into three categories:

- ➢ Infrastructure
- Chemicals
- Traditional Energy
- Property
- Mining
- Utilities
- Environment/New Energy
- Construction
- Logistics

- ➢ High-tech, manufacturing
- Telecom
- Semiconductors
- Electronics
- Internet/Software
- Automotive

- ➢ Consumer/leisure brands/services
- Finance
- Retail/Wholesale
- Entertainment
- Commercial Services
- Health

Although China officially began encouraging its businesses to go abroad back in the 1990s, the original wave of substantial Chinese investments in Europe before 2008 was mainly **opportunistic**. Chinese companies –both public and private- were interested in acquiring brands and technology. Good examples of this include Volvo of Sweden, acquired by a little-known private car manufacturer, Geely. State companies started to appear as prospective investors in Portugal, Italy, Greece, Germany, France in the early 2000s. This was before Xi Jinping became general secretary of the Chinese Communist Party, in October 2012. This year, Mr. Xi was reappointed as general secretary and also as State president. Meeting in March 2018, China's National People's Congress scrapped the two-term limit for presidential terms, potentially allowing him to stay in power beyond 2023.

2/ From "traditional" FDI to "Belt and Road" investments

In 2013 came the Belt and Road Initiative, a network of regional infrastructure projects including railways, roads, ports, airports, telecommunication links, oil and gas pipelines and energy facilities. Launched by Xi Jinping himself, the BRI is now the centerpiece of China's foreign and domestic policies.

Today, connections between existing Chinese investments in Europe and the BRI abound (although it is important to keep in mind that not all Chinese FDI is part of BRI). In the maritime domain, new port facilities and other coastal infrastructures built or acquired by Beijing extend from China to parts of Africa and the Mediterranean. In the context, the Piraeus Harbor becomes a key element of BRI and the acquisition of port facilities in the north of Europe would also make perfect sense for China. There are talks of railway connections between Greece and Central Europe, via the Balkans (especially Serbia), projects that would be conducive to BRI's end goal. That being said, their completion is still a way off, as there are many complexities in this region – as in many other parts of Europe.

Meanwhile, the fact that Chinese entities also partially or wholly own at least four airports (Heathrow, Manchester, Parma and Toulouse, where Airbus is headquartered), and six seaports is no coincidence. China has expressed interest in developing e-commerce across

Europe, and will need to expand logistical capacities, hence its acquisitions of massive land from Montenegro to Portugal, and from rural France to Poland and Hungary. Some additional docksides have been bought or leased. In some cases, they remain unused.

What will happen next?

BRI keeps expanding, with the criteria used to qualify a particular project in a particular country for inclusion in the program elastic and vague. The initiative also has no clear objective or timeframe, which leaves open whether China intends to use this plan to "rule the world," as author David Ignatius put it in a recent *New York Times* editorial[5]. Above all, it will be a long, painful march, especially once China realizes that dealing with so many countries and cultures – even over an indefinite period of time – is an almost impossible challenge.

There are already growing problems along the BRI. For example, reports have appeared about suspected tax fraud at Piraeus harbour, now run by a Chinese state-owned company, *Cosco*[6]. The European Anti-Fraud Office (OLAF) confirmed it is working with Italy on the investigation into the suspected tax scams, but declined to give details.

In Central and Eastern Europe, plans for a 350-km railway between Belgrade and Budapest have stalled for obscure reasons[7], most likely a violation by the Hungarian government of EU public procurement rules[8]. The project was supposed to symbolize the vibrant partnership between China and this region, and it is possible that Chinese companies are waiting for a more opportune time to progress.

Above all, China has so far failed to get a substantial number of Europeans interested in the BRI. Unlike in China itself, where BRI has become a household name, polls show a lack of knowledge about the initiative in most European countries. The leaders of Germany, the UK and France all skipped Beijing's Belt and Road Forum in Beijing in May 2017, as did the president of the European Commission. Instead the latter sent one of his vice-presidents, Jyrki Katainen, who said that any scheme connecting Europe and Asia should adhere to a number of principles, including market rules and international procurement standards, and should complement existing networks and policies. In fact, 27 EU ambassadors to Beijing have gone on record to criticize the Chinese plan, warning that it threatened to damage free trade.[9]

---

[5] David Ignatius: China has a plan to rule the world, Washington Post, November 28, 2017
https://www.washingtonpost.com/opinions/china-has-a-plan-to-rule-the-world/2017/11/28/214299aa-d472-11e7-a986-d0a9770d9a3e_story.html?noredirect=on&utm_term=.03f62d0dd700
[6] EU suspects tax fraud at China's new 'gateway to Europe' as state-owned shipping firm Cosco faces mounting opposition abroad, Reuters, April 20, 2018
[7] EU sets collision course with China over 'Silk Road' rail project, Financial Times, February 19, 2017
https://www.ft.com/content/003bad14-f52f-11e6-95ee-f14e55513608
[8] Unlike Serbia, Hungary is a member of the European Union and need to comply with the bloc's competition rules
[9] https://global.handelsblatt.com/politics/eu-ambassadors-beijing-china-silk-road-912258

As an alternative narrative to BRI, the EU plans to release this year a strategy on "Euro-Asian Connectivity", to promote cooperation on regional infrastructure between Europe and Asia in a way that upholds high standards and principles. The existing EU-China Connectivity Platform is already working to promote synergies between the BRI and EU policies and projects such as such as the Trans-European Transport Network Policy. The goal is to ensure that BRI is an "open platform which adheres to market rules and international norms[10]." The EU-China Connectivity Platform promotes cooperation on infrastructure, including financing, interoperability and logistics. The framework has already generated cooperation on various projects.

It is fair to say that the BRI presents opportunities for Europe, but it is primarily a Chinese project that will help China expand its influence in the Eurasian region and beyond. It is not clear what level of control China's "partners" will have. For the past few years, China has demonstrated its ability to divide Europeans by creating entities such as the 16+1 format, a group designed to facilitate government and business contacts between China and Eastern and Central Europe; and by encouraging EU members to join the Beijing-run Asian Infrastructure Investment Bank (AIIB).

Although connectivity is both a Chinese and an EU concept, it is easy to understand why certain European leaders are reluctant to give China carte blanche to invest in the continent's infrastructure. At the end of the day, Europe and China have similar aims in their respective territories: preserving jobs, fuelling economic growth, and maintaining social stability. However, they have different ways of pursuing these goals and may achieve them better by staying somewhat apart.

3/ The screening mechanism debate: not an "EU CFIUS"

The Committee on Foreign Investments in the United States (CFIUS) generally focuses on foreign investments in U.S. companies that could pose a risk to national security —meaning companies that do business with large firms with strategically important technologies. The ongoing congressional discussions, led by Sen. John Cornyn (R-Texas), aim to expand the scope of CFIUS and give it oversight over more types of transactions.

In Europe, several countries have developed their own mechanisms to screen foreign investments that directly impact the activities of defence ministries or security agencies, but only a few countries have put in place a systematic screening mechanism for foreign investments in technologies, infrastructure, or other key economic sectors. Even those few countries that do have a mechanism in place usually run an ad-hoc Cabinet-level process, handled by the national Ministry of Economics. Very few deals have been blocked, at least officially. A prominent exception was the 2017 attempted purchase of German semiconductor company *Aixtron* by *Fujian Grand Chip Investment Fund*, which was

---

[10] European Commission, "Joint Communication to the European Parliament and the Council Elements for a new EU strategy on China", JOIN (2016) 30 final, Brussels, June 22, 2016, http://eeas.europa.eu/archives/delegations/china/documents/more_info/eu_china_strategy_en.pdf

simultaneously blocked in Europe and in the United States, due to *Aixtron*'s American component. The French Finance Ministry has acknowledged having blocked "many deals".

As often, the answer lies in a joint European approach. In early 2017, the governments of Germany, France and Italy ignited a debate by sending a letter to the European Commission asking the EU to rethink rules on FDI. In his September 2017 state-of-the union address, Commission President Jean-Claude Juncker spoke out in favor of more investment screening measures against Chinese takeovers. "If a foreign state-owned company wants to purchase a European harbor, part of our energy infrastructure or a defense technology firm, this should only happen with transparency," he said. The nonbinding cooperation system between member states and the Union that Juncker proposed "can be activated when a specific foreign investment in one or several member states may affect the security or public order of another."[11] The planned framework would allow members to share details of proposed acquisitions on the grounds of security or public order, including those related to research, transport, energy or space.

A debate is now taking place in the European Parliament[12], between states that want Chinese investments to be screened —or at least to be examined in a transparent way- and EU members who have opposed or at least remained silent so as not to offend China, a major investor. Among the countries in favor are Germany, France, the UK, Italy, Spain, and Poland. Among those who are more critical of screening proposals are Finland, Greece, Hungary, the Czech Republic, Austria, and Malta.

Some governments, including those of Finland and Austria, have described such a procedure as "protectionist." Many others have remained silent.

In Central and Eastern Europe, many countries, including some[13] that are part of the so-called "16+1" group set up by China in 2011 in parallel to the EU, have mixed feelings about Brussels' plans. Heads of governments from the group will meet again in Sofia, Bulgaria in July 2019, (controversially immediately after the annual EU-China summit). Like Greece, several of these countries have been chastised by EU and German officials since the 2008 European debt crisis. They feel that Western Europe is not providing enough help to them. This sentiment is even stronger in the Balkans where candidate countries such as Serbia, Montenegro, and Albania are welcoming Chinese money warmly in a bid to boost their economies. Many have received substantial Chinese government loans or projects in exchange for open-door policies. China may be establishing its presence in this region in anticipation of these Balkan countries eventually joining the EU.

---

[11] State of the Union 2017 - Trade Package: European Commission proposes framework for screening of foreign direct investments, European Commission, September 14, 2017, http://europa.eu/rapid/press-release_IP-17-3183_en.htm

[12] Philippe Le Corre: EU nations must come together on Chinese investment, Nikkei Asian Review, October 11, 2017. https://asia.nikkei.com/Opinion/EU-nations-must-come-together-on-Chinese-investment2

[13] The 16 members are: Albania, Bosnia and Herzegovina, Bulgaria, Croatia, the Czech Republic, Estonia, Hungary, Latvia, Lithuania, Macedonia, Montenegro, Poland, Romania, Serbia, Slovakia, Slovenia

In acknowledging the interests of members like Greece and Hungary[14], the European commission is having to navigate between demonstrating that Europe is open for business and trying to implement the new investment screening framework. While French President Emmanuel Macron tries to initiate new EU reforms, there is no doubt that this topic will lead to further intra-European discussions. As the continent's economy improves, it is quite possible to envisage more cross-European investment in line with the "new EU" outlined in Macron's speech to the European Parliament in Strasbourg in April this year. But the EU will still need outside investors and, for many members, China will remain an appealing source of funds.

The issue of reciprocity

Year after year, the European Chamber of Commerce in China has pointed out the lack of market-access in China, while European markets have remained fairly open to foreign investment, including from China, leading to massive investments from Chinese actors. This lack of reciprocity has become a sticking point in EU-China relations.

Although major Chinese deals are taking place in Europe, many European companies are finding it more difficult than before to access the Chinese market. According to the Mercator Institute for China Studies (Merics), EU investments in China amounted to just $8 billion in 2016, one quarter the volume of Chinese investments in the EU[15]. The lack of investment reciprocity harms European interests and leads to the perception of China as a bad faith trade partner. Still, according to Merics, "the perception of China as a free rider undermines popular support for economic cooperation with China and for an open, liberal economic order in Western democracies". Since the start of China's "open-door policy" in the late 1970s, foreign companies in China have operated under a separate set of rules from domestic companies, and have been forced to set up joint-ventures with Chinese partners. Many foreign companies consider that they are being discriminated against. China continues to restrict foreign investment in such sectors as fisheries, media, communications, financial services, transport, electricity and construction.

This situation has affected the discussions between the EU and China on the signing of a much-needed Common Agreement on Investment, the equivalent of the, similarly delayed, U.S.-China bilateral investment agreement.

---

[14] There have also been foreign policy consequences: Last year, Greece blocked the issuance of an EU statement at the United Nations criticizing China's human-rights record. In July 2016, Hungary, Croatia and Greece —all concerned with territorial disputes, but also of not offending Beijing- opposed a strong statement by the EU's High representative for External affairs following a ruling by the Permanent Court of Arbitration in The Hague overwhelmingly in favour of the Philippines and against China, over claims to the South China Sea.

[15] Chinese FDI in Europe in 2017, Rapid recovery after initial slowdown, Merics, April 17, 2018. https://www.merics.org/en/papers-on-china/chinese-fdi-in-europe

As this author recommended in the past[16], the issue of reciprocity should also be tackled through transatlantic cooperation, in a process that could also include other Organisation for Economic Cooperation and Development (OECD) members. The National Security Strategy calls for dialogue with European allies to "contest China's unfair trade and economic practices and restrict its acquisition of sensitive technologies," but it is not clear whether the Trump Administration is advocating for a joint approach. The U.S. and the EU should ensure regular information-sharing and joint monitoring of the nature and extent of Chinese investments and economic activities in Europe. Although the U.S. and the EU do not always speak with one voice, they should coordinate and present a united front as Chinese capital continues to flow towards the European continent[17]. As a consequence of a possible tightening of foreign investment screening in the U.S. and a general worsening of U.S.-China relations, it is possible that Chinese capital originally destined to the U.S. will switch to the European continent, which makes transatlantic collaboration even more essential.

---

[16] *China's Global rise: can the U.S. and EU pursue a coordinated strategy?* Brookings Institution, Asia Working Papers, October 2016

[17] EU-China FDI: working towards reciprocity in investment relations, Merics, April 17, 2018

Mr. ROHRABACHER. Thank you very much, and we see about—we have next with us Gordon Chang is an author who has spent years living and working on—in China and in Hong Kong. He's the author of "The Coming Collapse of China" and is a columnist for the Daily Beast and frequently appears as a regular expert guest on various news programs.

Mr. Chang, go right ahead.

STATEMENT OF MR. GORDON CHANG, AUTHOR

Mr. CHANG. Chairman Rohrabacher, Ranking Member Meeks, and distinguished members of the committee, it's a great privilege for me to be here today and I thank you for this opportunity.

Europe is where China subverts our curbs on the acquisitions of sensitive technologies. Whether China is revolutionary or just merely revisionist—and I think it's revolutionary—but whatever it is, it has to dominate technology if it's going to realize its broad and ever expanding ambitions.

Xi Jinping, the Chinese ruler, has his Made in China 2025 Initiative, which seeks self-sufficiency in 10 critical sectors. It is the heart of his industrial policy, and his industrial policy is the heart of his plan to become the number-one economy.

Chairman Rohrabacher talked about China's predatory trade practices. Clearly, CM 2025, which the Chinese know it is a grand assault on the WTO.

Now, to achieve the goals that Xi Jinping has, one of them is to give assistance for the acquisition of foreign technology, and government support is probably the best reason why Midea Group, which is a home appliance maker—microwaves, air conditioners—why it, in 2016 and 2017, acquired Kuka A.G., which is Germany's foremost robotics company.

Yes, companies diversify all the time. But in this particular case where you see a company stray so far from its geographical area, so far from its core business that government direction is the best answer for why this occurred.

Beijing's preferred target, of course, is American technology and here, we've seen China, very shrewdly, invest in startups, also scoop up distressed American tech companies.

And Ranking Member Meeks talked about the changing mix of China's investments into Europe where you can see the changing mix in the United States as well with technology.

China's technology investments seem to have followed in the last half decade two things—first of all, the Made in China 2025 Initiative, plus, also China's two 5-year plans—the Twelfth and the Thirteenth.

Now, Chinese tech acquisitions in the U.S. have gotten harder. There have been more clamps on this. Ranking Member Meeks asked well, what can we do, and part of this is, you know, we have to see what the U.S. does and hopefully these lessons rub off on the Europeans as well.

So, for instance, in that Kuka acquisition, we did not stop it, as the United States might have been able to do because of our approval process.

But we did stop in December 2016 in one of the last acts of the Obama administration was the acquisition of a subsidiary of

Aixtron, the German chip equipment maker, and that, I think, was a very important turn because we see the Trump administration following that example with two disapprovals of Chinese acquisitions.

Interestingly, we see Shenzhen-based Huawei Technologies. It is the world's largest maker of telecom equipment. Because of its connections with the People's Liberation Army and with Chinese security services, it has largely been shut out of the American market, and that's a great thing.

But the one thing that Huawei has done is after being shut out of the U.S. it has moved into Europe and now derives something like 35 percent of its revenues from the continent.

We have seen other Chinese companies also adopt this "shun the U.S., embrace Europe" concept.

The Chinese are acquiring a lot. We heard from Mr. Le Corre some statistics from Bloomberg. What's fascinating is that in this 10-year period that Bloomberg refers to $318 billion worth of acquisitions in Europe, the Chinese have spent 45 percent more in Europe than they have in the United States, as they acquired 360 companies.

At this moment, as Chairman Rohrabacher mentions, there is no general screening process in the European Union, only, as you mentioned, 12 out of 28 EU countries have a screening process of their own.

The important thing here, I think, is that we are seeing France and Germany, which is the core of the economic union, is actually starting to think about screening.

We heard President Macron talk about "protective Europe" a couple months ago. And so this is going to be important. The other thing that we can do is set that example and here, I think, that we need to show the Europeans that we have the political will to stop Chinese investment because then, I think, they will, and that will be the example that you talk about, Chairman Meeks.

I didn't plan to speak about Lajes but it's something very close to my heart. Just before I run out of time, I want to mention that if the Chinese were to get the air base in Lajes, they would be able to be closer to Washington and New York than Pearl Harbor is to Los Angeles and San Francisco. That is something we cannot permit.

Thank you.

[The prepared statement of Mr. Chang follows:]

Statement of
Gordon G. Chang

Subcommittee on
Europe, Eurasia, and Emerging Threats
House Committee on Foreign Affairs

Chinese Investment and Influence in Europe

May 23, 2018

Chairman Rohrabacher, Ranking Member Meeks, and distinguished Members of the Committee:

It is a privilege for me to appear before you today, and I thank you for this opportunity.

My name is Gordon Guthrie Chang. I am a writer and live in Bedminster, New Jersey.

I worked as a lawyer in Hong Kong from 1981-1991 and in Shanghai from 1996-2001. Between these two periods, I frequently traveled to Asia from California. I regularly go to Asia now.

I am the author of *The Coming Collapse of China* (Random House, 2001) and *Nuclear Showdown: North Korea Takes On the World* (Random House, 2006).

I am a Daily Beast columnist and write for other publications from time to time. I concentrate on Asia, especially China and North Korea.

Conclusion

This testimony looks at how China views Europe, other than Russia, in the context of Beijing's attempts to dominate technology sectors.

I conclude that Europe is where China is trying to undermine the United States, especially subverting American curbs on acquisition of sensitive technologies.

Chinese Ambitions

Whether China is a "revisionist" or "revolutionary"[1] power, it will need to dominate technology if it is to realize its broad—and fast expanding—ambitions.

Xi Jinping, the Chinese ruler, has put technological dominance close to the top of his agenda. There is, most infamously, his Made in China 2025 initiative, which seeks self-sufficiency in ten sectors, such as aircraft, robotics, electric cars, and computer chips. An "updated national plan," released January of this year, emphasizes 5G, the next generation of wireless communications.

CM2025, as the initiative is known in China, is at the heart of Xi's industrial policy, and his industrial policy is at the heart of his plan to make China the world's technological leader and dominant economy. To achieve the goals of the plan, Beijing offers large low-interest loans from state investment funds and development banks; generous research subsidies; and, most relevant to this testimony, assistance for acquisitions of foreign technology.

This government support for acquisitions is certainly the best explanation of why Midea Group, a Chinese manufacturer of home appliances like air conditioners and microwave ovens, would purchase Kuka AG, known as Germany's foremost robotics company.

Companies diversify of course, but the takeover of a foreign concern that far afield from the acquirer's core business looks government-directed or at least motivated by government wishes, especially because the acquisition netted China a technology that had been targeted by Beijing's most important industrial policy.

In this case, a Chinese company had spare cash and Chinese technocrats saw an opportunity to act. In the absence of government support or involvement, it is extremely unlikely Midea would have even thought of going to the other end of the Eurasian landmass to buy a business so unrelated to its own.

CM2025's support for acquisitions of technology supplements Beijing's "Go Out" or "Go Global" strategy, an effort, dating to 1999, to encourage Chinese enterprises to acquire foreign businesses.

Takeovers of such businesses declined last year—outbound non-financial investment fell 29.4% according to China's Commerce Ministry.[2] Does this mean Beijing's support for foreign acquisitions is on the wane?

No. Chinese officials, worried about accelerating capital flight evident in 2015 and 2016, clamped down hard on acquisitions. The crackdown on capital movements, however, does not seem to have crimped the central government's effort to buy foreign technology.

Beijing's preferred target has been, of course, the United States of America. There, China has been shrewd in buying or funding start-ups and scooping up distressed U.S. tech companies.

In short, whether in Europe or the United States, much of the China's outbound investment in the past half-decade is in areas targeted by either Made in China 2025 or Beijing's 12th and 13th Five-Year Plans, which together cover the decade ending 2020.

American Response

China's ambitions, backed by its state-directed campaign, worry American policymakers. Zheng Yongnian of the National University of Singapore maintains the West is on "high alert" on China, believing, in the words of the *South China Morning Post*, that "the U.S. was launching a technology cold war against the country."[3]

"Cold war" is an overstatement. Although there have been some U.S. prohibitions on Chinese tech acquisitions, China has mostly been able to buy what it wants. American officials, for instance, did not block Midea's suspicious purchase of Kuka, as they had the power to do.[4]

Nonetheless, it is true Chinese tech acquisitions in the U.S. have become harder as a practical matter in the last couple years. In high-profile cases, U.S. authorities have sometimes stopped Chinese money from scooping up American technology.

Presidents Obama and Trump, for example, used their power to derail large deals. In December 2016, Obama by executive order implemented the recommendation of the Committee on Foreign Investment in the United States and blocked a $723 million Chinese bid to purchase Aixtron, a German-based concern making equipment used in fabricating semiconductors. The prohibition was only the third time an American president had implemented a recommendation from CFIUS, as the interagency committee is commonly called, to stop a transaction.

The fourth and fifth times came in the Trump administration. Trump in September of his first year in office prevented Canyon Bridge Capital Partners, a Chinese-controlled buyout fund, from taking over chipmaker Lattice Semiconductor Corp. Then in March of this year the president ordered Broadcom, then a Singapore-incorporated company, to drop efforts to buy Qualcomm, the San Diego-based chipmaker.

The later action was especially noteworthy because, although none of the parties were Chinese, Trump had China in mind while ordering the prohibition. A Broadcom victory in a hostile contest was considered to also be a victory for China. Why? If successful, the Singapore company, in an effort to lift shareholder value, would almost certainly have sold off Qualcomm assets quickly, reduced R&D budgets substantially, and controlled costs ruthlessly. That would have pleased markets but made it difficult, as a practical matter, for the U.S. to compete in the global race for 5G.[5]

With Qualcomm out of the 5G race, China's Huawei Technologies, which receives substantial backing from Beijing, would have been able to set global standards and end up the world's 5G provider. As the Broadcom-Qualcomm battle shows, these days any transaction having China implications is going to get a thorough CFIUS review. Bloomberg reports that CFIUS concerns have led to the abandonment of several technology deals as the Trump administration moves with determination to protect American innovation.[6]

As it should. There is pending legislation, sponsored by Senator John Cornyn, the Texas Republican, to expand CFIUS's authority. "CFIUS needs to get much smarter and more agile," Alan Tonelson told Fox News in early March. "Regimes like China's nowadays can access knowhow through multiple channels both direct and indirect. CFIUS's mandate needs to be flexible enough to cover all those currently existing and new schemes as they emerge."[7]

Due to its recent activity, CFIUS has become one of Beijing's targets recently. The *Washington Post* reported this month that Beijing had handed U.S. trade negotiators a list of its "economic and trade demands."[8] Many of those demands, when read together, told the Trump administration it had to drop restrictions on acquisition of U.S. technology. "They expect to be treated the same way our treaty allies are treated, which is ridiculous," Derek Scissors of the American Enterprise Institute told the paper, speaking of the Chinese.

In the atmosphere in Washington these days, that demand, in Scissors's words, is "crazy," and the Chinese know it, which is why they have instead been trying to buy European tech, in many cases comparable to America's. The stakes for the United States are enormous because the success of its export-control regime depends on getting European capitals to control tech transfers, by acquisition or otherwise.

The risk is not theoretical, unfortunately, and Shenzhen-based Huawei, the world's leading telecom-equipment maker, is a case in point. The company, thought to have close linkages with China's People's Liberation Army and the Chinese security services, is being shut out of the U.S. market due to national security concerns.

Yet Huawei has been able to bypass America. The fast-growing Chinese company "has invested billions across the Continent" and now derives a stunning 35% of its revenues from Europe.[9] Huawei, in comparison to its fortunes in the United States, "has had better luck in Europe."[10] And Huawei is not the only Chinese company to adopt a shun-U.S.-embrace-Europe strategy.[11]

European Response

Of course, China is getting European tech in many ways, one being through European investment into China. In China, of course, intellectual property is either stolen or lost through leaching.

In this regard, on May 18 Xinhua News Agency announced that two entities in Chengdu, the Chengdu High-Tech Industrial Development Zone and China Taiping Investment Holdings, established a fund of 1 billion yuan ($157 million) for the purpose of "technology transfer and achievement transformation between China and the EU." The choice of the city is significant because Chengdu is making itself into a technology center for Europe. It is, for instance, the site of the EU-China Business and Technology Cooperation Fair, which has already had 12 sessions.[12]

European companies, like their American counterparts, are wary of transferring their best tech to China, so the greater concern for the U.S. is Chinese acquisition of Europe's best tech by buying European companies. The Chinese are acquiring a lot, and the pace is accelerating fast.

According to Bloomberg News's most recent calculations, Chinese parties have purchased or invested at least $318 billion in Europe during the last 10 years. China has poured 45% more into Europe than in the U.S. during the period. China, the news organization notes, has acquired 360 European companies since 2008.[13]

Chinese investment, despite the recent downturn caused by tightened capital controls, is on a general upswing. As Bloomberg reports, "2016 was by far the biggest year for Chinese dealmaking in Europe."[14]

Another source highlights the big increase in China's commitment to the Continent: Chinese foreign direct investment into Europe in 2010 was 1.6 billion euros, rising to 35 billion euros in 2016.[15]

The mix of Chinese investments is also changing. Investment in tech, undoubtedly due to Beijing's direction, is on the rise. "In the early years, Chinese investors took advantage of the benefits the less-developed southern European economies could provide and invested in a wide range of sectors, from real estate to entertainment," writes Magda Tsakalidou, an analyst studying Chinese investment patterns in Europe. "Now, their investment policy has become more strategically planned, aiming at long-term national benefits. Chinese investors are redirecting their efforts to the three major European economies—Germany, the U.K., and France—and targeting manufacturing enterprises and high-tech firms."[16] Some add Italy to that group.[17]

As Tsakalidou notes, China's relatively recent move to buy European tech has concerned the Continent's leaders.[18]

The latest U.S. National Security Strategy, issued by the Trump administration in December, states "China is gaining a strategic foothold in Europe" by, among other tactics, "investing in key industries, sensitive technologies, and infrastructure."[19]

That strategic foothold should not be a surprise. Europe does not have a tech-control regime.

Europe, however, is struggling to develop one. An EU Commission paper, issued May 2017, stated "concerns have recently been voiced about foreign investors, notably state-owned enterprises, taking over European companies with key technologies for strategic reasons."[20] Little, however, has been done to address those concerns, even after Midea's early 2017 purchase of Kuka.[21]

Germany, the home of Kuka, along with France and Italy wanted EU leaders at a June 2017 EU Council summit to call on the EU Commission to consider "ways to screen investments from third countries." Although the three countries managed to get their language into draft statements, the final version of the summit document did not include their proposal. Smaller states, which had benefitted from Chinese investment, blocked the initiative.[22]

A draft EU Commission regulation, released in September of last year, would permit the Commission to screen for "security and public order" that was "likely to affect projects or programs of EU interest." The regulation, however, would not give the Commission the power to block an investment.[23]

At the moment, only 12 of the 28 EU member states have screening rules.[24]

Incidentally, Europe is the number one destination for Chinese investment in part because it does not have a mechanism in place to stop foreign investment.[25] So Europe is the gaping hole in American efforts to stop the flow of tech to China.

The EU, with so many member states and its unanimity rule, is particularly susceptible to Beijing's divide-and-conquer strategy. China, by dividing and conquering, has been able to get what it wants, at least most of the time.

There are reasons for hope, however. First, the two core members of the EU are especially concerned about protecting European innovation from Chinese acquisition. French President Emmanuel Macron publicly advanced the notion of a "protective Europe"[26] in the context of the security threatened by China's investments. He did not get his way in EU councils, as evident from recent events, but he has not given up.

Moreover, Macron has an important ally, German Chancellor Angela Merkel. Her vice chancellor, Sigmar Gabriel raised the reciprocity point that has gained traction in the

United States, recently stating his country should not sacrifice "its companies on the altar of free markets" while Beijing shuts German companies out of the Chinese market.[27]

So while Beijing has been looking for and found its "points of entrée" in the eastern and southeastern EU member states, the heart of the organization—where much of the valuable technology is found—is putting up a stout defense.

And that defense is urgently needed. As Bloomberg notes about Chinese investment, "More than half of the known investment total is concentrated in Europe's five largest economies."[28]

Second, what European countries will not protect, the United States will. As mentioned above, the Obama administration blocked China's bid for Aixtron. Specifically, the U.S. in December 2016 refused to permit the transfer of a U.S.-incorporated subsidiary to a German sub controlled by China's Fujian Grand Chip Investment Fund. Prior to Obama's action, Berlin withdrew approval for the acquisition, but only after Washington had urged it to do so.[29]

So American administrations can, as a practical matter, prevent Chinese takeovers of some European tech-heavy companies, and in other cases the U.S. can stop or at least control such acquisitions through export-controls on licenses of American tech.

American Political Will

"We will work with our partners to contest China's unfair trade and economic practices and restrict its acquisition of sensitive technologies," the 2017 National Security Strategy states.[30]

Working with partners, European and otherwise, has not always been easy when the issue is China. As an initial matter, the issue is not whether America has the leverage over Europe to stop Chinese acquisitions of European technology. The issue is whether Washington has the political will to use that power. Political will, to a great extent, is the result of perceptions of the harm China can do with its possession of technology. Many, unfortunately, see China as benign.

China is not. By now, political leaders on both sides of the Atlantic should realize that Beijing is absolutely determined to control technology and will stop at little to obtain it. And it is up to the United States to figure out strategies, both hard and soft, to get Europe to plug the hole through which tech is pouring out of the West into the hands of a rapacious China.

---

[1]   Xi Jinping looks like he wants to replace the current international system with a China-centric order. *See* Gordon G. Chang, "Trump's 'Beautiful Vision' vs. China's Imperial Dream," National Interest, December 27, 2017, http://nationalinterest.org/feature/trumps-%E2%80%98beautiful-vision%E2%80%99-vs-chinas-imperial-dream-23826.

[2]   "China's Outbound Investment Slumped in 2017 as Deals Scrutinized," Bloomberg News, January 16, 2018, https://www.bloomberg.com/news/articles/2018-01-16/china-s-outbound-investment-slumped-in-2017-as-deals-scrutinized.

[3]   Wendy Wu and Robert Delaney, " 'It's Not Over Yet': Key Sticking Points Remain for US and China on Trade, Analysts Say," *South China Morning Post* (Hong Kong), May 21, 2018, http://www.scmp.com/news/china/diplomacy-defence/article/2146983/its-not-over-yet-key-sticking-points-remain-us-and?from=groupmessage&isappinstalled=0. China's moving up the tech scale has alarmed American and European officials. *See, e.g.*, Thomas L. Friedman, "The U.S. and China Are Finally Having It Out," *New York Times*, May 1, 2018, https://www.nytimes.com/2018/05/01/opinion/america-china-trump-trade.html.

[4]   *See* "China's Midea Receives U.S. Green Light for Kuka Takeover," Reuters, December 30, 2016, https://www.reuters.com/article/us-kuka-m-a-mideamidea-group-idUSKBN14J0SP.

[5]   *See* Gordon G. Chang, "Why the Bid to Buy Qualcomm Poses a Dire Threat to US National Security," Fox News Opinion, March 2, 2018, http://www.foxnews.com/opinion/2018/03/02/why-bid-to-buy-qualcomm-poses-dire-threat-to-us-national-security.html.

[6]   *See* David McLaughlin, "Trump Blocks Broadcom Takeover of Qualcomm on Security Risks," Bloomberg Politics, March 12, 2018, https://www.bloomberg.com/news/articles/2018-03-12/trump-issues-order-to-block-broadcom-s-takeover-of-qualcomm-jeoszwnt.

[7]   Chang, "Why the Bid to Buy Qualcomm Poses a Dire Threat to US National Security."

[8]   Josh Rogin, "China Gave Trump a List of Crazy Demands, and He Caved to One of Them," *Washington Post*, May 15, 2018, https://www.washingtonpost.com/news/josh-rogin/wp/2018/05/15/china-gave-trump-a-list-of-crazy-demands-and-he-caved-to-one-of-them/?utm_term=.45bb5b2c98d9.

[9]   Laurens Cerulus, "Europe Turns Cool on Chinese Tech," Politico Europe, May 9, 2018, https://www.politico.eu/article/europe-reaches-moment-of-reckoning-over-5g-security-huawei-us-donald-trump-cybersecurity/.

[10]   Yukon Huang, "Why China Invests More in Europe Than in the US," *Financial*

Times (London), July 24, 2017, https://www.ft.com/content/a7641d16-6c66-11e7-b9c7-15af748b60d0.

[11]   *See, e.g.*, Daniel Ren, "Chinese State Investment Firm to Avoid US and Look to Europe in Pursuit of Tech Assets as Trade Row Deepens," *South China Morning Post* (Hong Kong), April 5, 2018 (China Jianyin Investment, an equity investment vehicle), http://www.scmp.com/business/companies/article/2140369/chinese-state-investment-firm-avoid-us-trade-row-deepens-and-look.

[12]   "First EU-China Tech Scale-Up Summit Yields Fruit," Xinhua News Agency, May 18, 2018, http://www.xinhuanet.com/english/2018-05/18/c_137189707.htm.

[13]   Andre Tartar, Mira Rojanasakul, and Jeremy Scott Diamond, "How China Is Buying Its Way into Europe," Bloomberg News, April 23, 2018, https://www.bloomberg.com/graphics/2018-china-business-in-europe/.

[14]   Ibid.

[15]   *See* Friso Stevens, "Europe Ponders How to Curb China's High-Tech Buying Spree," Diplomat, February 16, 2018, https://thediplomat.com/2018/02/europe-ponders-how-to-curb-chinas-high-tech-buying-spree/.

[16]   Magda Tsakalidou, "Has Winter Come for Chinese Investments in the EU?" Diplomat, October 24, 2017, https://thediplomat.com/2017/10/has-winter-come-for-chinese-investments-in-the-eu/.

[17]   *See, e.g.*, Stevens, "Europe Ponders How to Curb China's High-Tech Buying Spree."

[18]   Tsakalidou, "Has Winter Come for Chinese Investments in the EU?"

[19]   "National Security Strategy of the United States of America," December 2017, https://www.whitehouse.gov/wp-content/uploads/2017/12/NSS-Final-12-18-2017-0905.pdf.

[20]   EU Commission, "Reflection Paper on Harnessing Globalisation," May 10, 2017, https://ec.europa.eu/commission/sites/beta-political/files/reflection-paper-globalisation_en.pdf.

[21]   Midea's purchase triggered concerns among European policymakers and leaders. *See, e.g.*, Tsakalidou, "Has Winter Come for Chinese Investments in the EU?"

[22]   Congressional Research Service, memorandum to House Subcommittee on Europe, Eurasia, and Emerging Threats, May 15, 2018.

[23]   Ibid.

24   Stevens, "Europe Ponders How to Curb China's High-Tech Buying Spree."

25   Tartar, Rojanasakul, and Diamond, "How China Is Buying Its Way into Europe."

26   Arthur Beesley, "Macron and Allies Head for EU Clash on Foreign Takeovers," *Financial Times* (London), June 15, 2017, https://www.ft.com/content/73aadc3a-5118-11e7-bfb8-997009366969.

27   Janosch Delcker, "Sigma Gabriel's Mission to Halt China's Investment Spree," Politico Europe, November 2, 2016, https://www.politico.eu/article/sigmar-gabriels-mission-to-halt-chinas-investment-spree/.

28   Tartar, Rojanasakul, and Diamond, "How China Is Buying Its Way into Europe."

29   *See* Maria Sheahan, "China's Fujian Drops Axitron Bid After Obama Blocks Deal," Reuters, December 8, 2016, https://www.reuters.com/article/us-aixtron-m-a-fujian/chinas-fujian-drops-aixtron-bid-after-obama-blocks-deal-idUSKBN13X16H.

30   National Security Strategy of the United States of America.

Mr. ROHRABACHER. Thank you very much.

And we have Mr. Kevin Freeman. He is an expert on global capital markets and is the CEO of Cross-Consulting and Services—an investment advisory firm.

He is also the author of several books, including "Economic Warfare: Risks and Responses," analysis of the 21st century risks in light of the recent market collapse, and many other things that you have written.

So we welcome your testimony today. You may proceed.

STATEMENT OF MR. KEVIN D. FREEMAN, AUTHOR

Mr. FREEMAN. Thank you, Mr. Chairman. Thank you, Ranking Member Reeks. My background—and thank you to the subcommittee.

My background, as you mentioned, Mr. Chairman, is international investing. I went to work for the great John Templeton in 1990.

Sir John Templeton truly pioneered global investing. He was a brilliant man, and I remember well—worked with him—being with him when the wall was coming down in Berlin, and we looked at that and I said, so where do you think the best place to invest would be—should we invest in Russia.

And he said no, we should invest in China, and the reason that he said that was he said the Chinese will remember how markets operate and they will be able to effectively operate in markets.

The Russians, on the other hand, were so far from a market economy that it would be a long learning process before they'd be successful.

Now, I thought that was interesting because at the time, in 1990, the Russian—the Soviet Union economy was number three in the world, second to the United States, and the Chinese economy wasn't ranked in the top ten.

Now we are here, just three decades later—less than three decades later—and China's economy is by some measures the largest in the world, if you follow purchasing power parity, and it is, clearly, at least second to ours.

So I understand global investments from the financial markets perspective and what Sir John Templeton taught me. But I also studied economic warfare, and in 2008 I was hired by the SOLIC Group in the Pentagon—Special Operations Low Intensity Conflict—to study irregular warfare and the role that economic warfare may have played in the 2008 financial collapse.

I believe it's necessary that we both have an understanding of global investing and economic warfare if you want to understand why and how of Chinese investing.

I want you to clearly understand that unlike Sir John Templeton, whose primary purpose in making an investment was the return to the investor, Chinese investments are not made with economic purposes—certainly, that they're a consideration but they're not the primary consideration.

This is true for not only China but all sovereign wealth funds. There is a national interest whenever a sovereign wealth fund invests. But it's particularly true for the Chinese.

It's also true for any Chinese individual investors who are scrutinized by the government for their investments as well as any companies in China which are many, in many cases, largely controlled by the People's Liberation Army or the state.

President Xi has announced himself President for life, essentially, and he's been jailing rivals, and what we see as a marketplace our enemies view as a battle space, and I believe that's particularly true with the Chinese.

One of the books that I've closely studied is a book titled "Unrestricted Warfare." It was published in 1999 by two senior colonels of the People's Liberation Army, and it outlines a series of efforts including hacking, influence operations, intellectual property theft, infiltration of leadership, currency warfare, and it alludes to things like the Confucius Institutes and the mass push of Chinese students into our colleges and universities, all of which are soft means of warfare.

I would suggest, to this committee, that Chinese investments must be seen from that perspective. I believe that this is a part, and my colleagues mentioned the Made in China 2025 policy, which is designed to have Chinese—China self-sufficient in certain industries and areas, I believe that too is a form of economic warfare and I believe all of this is a part of the 100-year marathon.

I brought a book from my friend, Mike Pillsbury, who wrote about the 100-year marathon and I would point you to the fact that in 1949 the People's Republic of China was formed, and 100 years from that period would be 2049.

This is an important date to recognize because the Chinese have learned from the Tiananmen Square incident in 1989 that 20 years later they were able to host the Olympics in Beijing.

So the belief, as I understand it in China, is that within two decades that you can remove a massacre and a horrific event from the world's consciousness and memory, therefore, if the goal is to have, essentially, the largest economy and the most powerful position in the world by 2049, the idea would be that you have to be completed with your horrific activity by the year 2029.

So I would suggest that over the next decade we will see a more aggressive China than we have seen in the past.

We are already beginning to see this. I was reading some Australian press reports complaining about the nations around Australia feeling Chinese influence following the acceptance of Chinese investments. And the Australians were wondering why are they no longer our friends—why are they becoming more China's friends.

I would also point to the effort starting in 2013 where the Chinese talked about de-Americanizing the world, removing the dollar as the world's primary reserve currency.

And we have seen an increase step-up in aggressive behavior since that day. I would point to recent press reports where something as simple as t-shirts sold at the Gap were questioned by China and therefore pulled because they happened to mention Tibet or Taiwan.

And a Canada Air travel magazine was recently pulled because Canada Air was told it is unacceptable to show Taiwan on a map in your travel magazine when you're flying.

I want to suggest, therefore, that the Chinese view this as wholly economic warfare. Every investment that they make is viewed from that perspective and we, unfortunately, as Americans, tend to view investments purely from an economic perspective. We must change that. We must reconnect the idea of national security and economics. They have been separated since the Clinton administration after the wall fell in Berlin.

Our nation said we have the most dominant military on the planet and we have the strongest economy and we said, go for it. And in both cases, we pursued military and economic goals. But they were no longer connected, which is a tremendous disservice to our national policy. We must reconnect it.

We must realize China is more than a competitor. They're, clearly, an adversary. We must do things like strengthen CFIUS, the Committee on Foreign Investment in the United States.

We must look beyond the political narrative—Democrat, Republican, left, right—and recognize that China is truly an adversary and we must carefully prepare for it.

We have largely ignored most of the economic warfare attacks, many of the things that I reported to the Pentagon in 2008, including the fact that Russia undertook what's known as a bear raid attack on our economy in the summer of 2008, time to disrupt our election.

I hear lots of discussion about Russia's involvement in the election of 2016. But when I was warning this Congress and the Pentagon and the FBI and the Defense Intelligence Agency and others that Russia was heavily involved in disrupting our economy just prior to election, most of my concerns were overlooked because, well, we don't really think in those terms.

We must think in those terms if we are going to succeed as a nation for the next several decades.

And so with that, I thank you for the opportunity to be here.

[The prepared statement of Mr. Freeman follows:]

Written Testimony of Kevin D. Freeman, CFA
U.S. House of Representatives Committee on Foreign Affairs
Subcommittee on Europe, Eurasia, and Emerging Threats
"Chinese Investment and Influence in Europe"
23 May 2018

Chairman Rohrabacher, Ranking Member Meeks, and Members of the Subcommittee, thank you for the opportunity to provide testimony regarding Chinese Investment and Influence in Europe.

My name is Kevin Freeman, and I have a background in global investment management with a Chartered Financial Analyst (CFA) designation. I am also an active student of Economic Warfare techniques, having written two books on the subject and providing research and testimony to the Department of Defense and various government agencies. I would like to begin with the proposition that what we see as a marketplace, our enemies view as a battlespace. When we recognize this truth, we will be better able to confront both opportunities and threats as they appear.

Early in my investment career, I had the privilege of working for Sir John Templeton, founder of the Templeton Funds and truly the pioneer of global investing. I met him in 1987 and went to work for him in 1990, as the world was dramatically shifting. These were glorious times for global investors as the Cold War was ending and there were amazing opportunities for profit emerging around the globe.

I well recall the time with Sir John when we were watching the fall of the Soviet Union. Despite the euphoria and consensus, he pointed me to China as the better investment. He said that because communism infected Russia in 1917 there were too few Russians alive who understood market behavior. By contrast, though, the Chinese fell to communism after the end of World War II. The Chinese thus had a better collective memory of how markets work. In hindsight, of course, he was right. In 1990, the Chinese economy wasn't listed among the world's top 10 when ranked by total Gross Domestic Product while the Soviet Union was ranked number 3. Now, less than three decades later, China is ranked second only to the United States in nominal GDP and by some estimates, using Purchasing Power Parity, is already the world's largest economy. Russia has fallen out of the top 10 entirely.[1] I make this point to demonstrate that the Chinese people understand the power of economics and, to borrow a phrase, the Art of a Deal.

---

[1] En.wikipedia.org. (2018). *List of countries by largest historical GDP*. [online] Available at: https://en.wikipedia.org/wiki/List_of_countries_by_largest_historical_GDP [Accessed 22 May 2018].

Investing in China, however, notoriously comes with a price. There are limits to capital flows in and out of China and limits on foreign ownership of Chinese assets.[2] Similarly, Chinese foreign investment also comes with a price. It is essential to remember that although China has instituted multiple market reforms over the past two decades, they overall remain a centrally planned economy. The markets are a tool of the state. And, all market-driven decisions are subject to review and oversight to make certain they strategically fit China-first priorities such as "Made in China 2025."[3] Investments often also require that intellectual property and control are transferred to Beijing.

To understand China, you must understand *The China Dream* as the goal and *Unrestricted Warfare* as the primary strategy.[4] *Unrestricted Warfare* is the title of a 1999 book written by two Senior PLA Colonels, Qiao Lang and Wang Xiangsui, published by the People's Liberation Army (PLA) Press. The concept of this book fits with near perfect accuracy the path of China over the two decades since it was published. Therefore, I strongly recommend to the Committee that any study of Chinese investments in Europe or elsewhere by considered through the lens of Unrestricted Warfare. This is, in essence, a view of global economic warfare.

Consider this quote from the English translation:

> "When people begin to lean toward and rejoice in the reduced use of military force to resolve conflicts, war will be reborn in another form and in another arena, becoming an instrument of enormous power in the hands of those who harbor intentions of controlling other countries or regions."[5]

If we had taken to heart the message of *Unrestricted Warfare* in 1999, we would have been quick to recognize the focus on Intellectual Property theft, hacking, currency manipulation, strategic control of rare earth minerals, satellite warfare, strategic acquisitions, financial market manipulation, and a host of other challenges that we see in place today. At the time, however, the focus was on opening Chinese markets for American business and rushing China into Most Favored Nation (MFN) status and the World Trade Organization (WTO). The political class, for the most part, even seemed willing to overlook clear Chinese efforts to influence our elections with massive illegal contributions. There was greater public evidence of Chinese interference in

---

[2] Ft.com. (2018). *China steps up capital controls with overseas withdrawal cap.* [online] Available at: https://www.ft.com/content/b69166fa-ee01-11e7-b220-857e26d1aca4 [Accessed 22 May 2018].

[3] Csis.org. (2018). *Made in China 2025.* [online] Available at: https://www.csis.org/analysis/made-china-2025 [Accessed 22 May 2018].

[4] BBC News. (2018). *What does Xi Jinping's China Dream mean?* [online] Available at: http://www.bbc.com/news/world-asia-china-22726375 [Accessed 22 May 2018].

[5] Qiao, L., Santoli, A. and Wang, X. (1999). *Unrestricted warfare.* Beijing: PLA Press

the 1996 election than anything demonstrated so far regarding Russia in 2016. In fact, there was clear evidence of foreign economic warfare in 2008 (although not Chinese) just before our Presidential election. I personally believe the outcome was dramatically altered as a result.

It is important to note that the Chinese authors were quite open about how they would exploit the weapons of Unrestricted Warfare while Americans remained in ignorance:

> "…the Americans have not been able to get their act together in this area. This is because proposing a new concept of weapons does not require relying on the springboard of new technology, it just demands lucid and incisive thinking. However, this is not a strong point of the Americans, who are slaves to technology in their thinking. The Americans invariably halt their thinking at the boundary where technology has not yet reached."[6]

The authors are basically suggesting that Americans see war as solely kinetic with the intention of direct physical destruction. Further, they are suggesting that the military of the United States is almost exclusively focused on personnel and equipment, on traditional weapons such as ships, planes, tanks, and missiles. *Unrestricted Warfare* requires looking beyond the military and kinetic and includes causing riots, a stock market crash, or acquiring a strategic port through purchase, as "new concept weapons." Further, they are direct in suggesting that Americans won't recognize such activity as warfare even while it is occurring before their very eyes.

After more than a decade of effort to inform policymakers and political leaders, I can sadly report that the Chinese author's assessment is largely correct.[7] For the last decade, I have been presenting clear and compelling evidence of economic warfare attacks against the United States. These attacks utilize new concept weaponry specifically listed in the *Unrestricted Warfare* doctrine. Yet, because my warnings did not fit the political narrative at the time, they were largely ignored and, in some cases, purposely suppressed.

A major problem is that we are siloed in our thinking. After declaring victory in the Cold War, we largely separated economics from defense. The belief was that we had the world's most capable military and global markets should be free and open. While both thoughts were (and are) mostly true in concept, the real-world application is actually quite different. Other than attempts to restrict terrorist financing or the use of sanctions to modify behavior, we have largely ignored the growing global economic war. In briefing after briefing to the Defense Intelligence establishment, I was told that while "these concerns are valid," they "were not in our swimming lanes" and thus remain unaddressed. The warfighters deigned ignorance of

---

[6] Qiao, L., Santoli, A. and Wang, X. (1999). *Unrestricted warfare*. Beijing: PLA Press

[7] The American Legion. (2012). *The message no one wanted to hear.* [online] Available at: https://www.legion.org/magazine/162503/message-no-one-wanted-hear [Accessed 22 May 2018].

markets and economics while the economists and financial community looked for profit opportunities, overlooking obvious geostrategic risks. These are the capitalists about whom the communists once boasted, "would sell the rope with which they hang us."

The Communist Chinese do not suffer under these same considerations. All actions are perceived from a geostrategic view. Dissent is not allowed. The time horizon is measured in decades, rather than with quarterly profits. Business and the military are greatly integrated. In fact, the PLA owns or controls a very large portion of Chinese business interests. The goal is not to maximize money but rather to reestablish China's rightful place in the world from their viewpoint. And their strategy roughly follows *Unrestricted Warfare*. This is obvious when you review inside documents not intended for Western eyes.

It is essential to recognize just how broad the nature of *Unrestricted Warfare* truly is. The range of influence operations from Hollywood to Washington is really quite extraordinary. I've included an Infographic from the *Epoch Times* that details these activities.[8] There should be no doubt that the "One Belt, One Road" efforts taking place in Europe and Asia are intimately tied to the same strategy.[9] Likewise, investments in Latin America and Africa are also part and parcel of *Unrestricted Warfare* and must be recognized as such.

For too long, the Chinese have been effective at hiding their true intentions, or "crossing the sea in full view" as ancient Chinese folklore would implore. As Dr. Michael Pillsbury explained in his powerful book, *The Hundred-Year Marathon*, "Americans have been wrong about China again and again, sometimes with profound consequences."[10] He should know as he admittedly was a leading "Panda Hugger" through multiple administrations dating back to Nixon. He has since understood the true nature of Chinese intentions.

As Confucius supposedly said, "there cannot be two suns in the sky." The goal under President Xi is to displace the United States so that China can take her rightful place, controlling at least one-third of the world's economy and overseeing the rest. The goal is to achieve this objective by 2049, 100 years after Mao took control. In addition, the Chinese realize that two decades after Tiananmen Square, the world celebrated China at the Beijing Olympics. The Chinese belief is that even horrendous action can be forgotten in 20 years. We should therefore expect Chinese belligerence between 2019 and 2029.

---

[8] www.theepochtimes.com. (2018). *Infographic: China's Secret War Against America* [online] Available at: https://www.theepochtimes.com/infographic-chinas-secret-war-against-america_2458236.html [Accessed 22 May 2018].

[9] Shin Kawashima, T. (2018). *The Risks of One Belt, One Road for China's Neighbors* [online] The Diplomat. Available at: https://thediplomat.com/2018/04/the-risks-of-one-belt-one-road-for-chinas-neighbors/ [Accessed 22 May 2018].

[10] Pillsbury, M. (2016). *The hundred-year marathon*. New York, New York: Griffin. Page 4

We are already witnessing an increasingly assertive China. Foreign companies that fail to conform to the Chinese purpose are criticized and punished. Most recently, Canada Air was called to account for the crime of publishing a map including Taiwan.[11] The Gap clothing store received Chinese anger for daring to sell a shirt that mentioned Tibet.[12] A report in Australia documents that Australia's neighbors are forced to adopt Chinese policy because they took Chinese investments, loans, and assistance.[13]

For those who doubt that *Unrestricted Warfare* has become the primary strategy to achieve Chinese dominance over America, I'd point you to Major General Gen. Qiao Liang. He was one of the two primary authors of *Unrestricted Warfare* in 1999. He now teaches at PLA National Defense University. Here is a recent quote from him in an Op-Ed he published in China Military Online:

> ***"To effectively contain the United States, other countries shall think more about how to cut off the capital flow to the United States..."[14]***

This was not intended for a Western audience but nonetheless provides a summary of Chinese strategy. We are now closing in on a period in which action will be increasingly overt and aggressive. The Chinese leadership believes that it is less necessary to conceal activity and can openly challenge the Western powers. A perfect example of this is President Xi's consolidation of power, jailing rivals, and appointing himself essentially "president for life." Another example is the official policy statement that China is calling for the "de-Americanization of the world."

We are now entering a critical phase in our relationship with China. The Chinese view themselves ascendant and expect the demise of American power. In fact, they are actively pursuing that outcome through Unrestricted Warfare. All investments, whether in Europe, Asia, Africa, or Latin America must be understood through this lens. All investments in the United States should be reviewed carefully by a strengthened CFIUS. Those firms with ties to the

---

[11] The Globe and Mail. (2018). *Air Canada bows to China, upsets Taiwan over Taipei relisting.* [online] Available at: https://www.theglobeandmail.com/politics/article-air-canada-begins-listing-taipei-as-part-of-china/ [Accessed 22 May 2018].

[12] Denyer, S. (2018). *Gap apologizes to China over map on T-shirt that omits Taiwan, South China Sea.* [online] Washington Post. Available at: https://www.washingtonpost.com/news/worldviews/wp/2018/05/15/u-s-retailer-gap-apologizes-to-china-over-map-on-t-shirt-that-omits-taiwan-south-china-sea/?utm_term=.097faca3b6a6 [Accessed 22 May 2018].

[13] Shin Kawashima, T. (2018). The Risks of One Belt, One Road for China's Neighbors. Retrieved from https://thediplomat.com/2018/04/the-risks-of-one-belt-one-road-for-chinas-neighbors/

[14] www.theepochtimes.com. (2016). *Chinese General Says 'Contain the United States' by Attacking Its Finances.* [online] Available at: https://www.theepochtimes.com/chinese-general-says-contain-the-united-states-by-attacking-its-finances_1967150.html [Accessed 22 May 2018].

People's Liberation Army should be especially scrutinized. And, all American investments in China should likewise be available for review. Peter Schweizer's sobering new book, *Secret Empires*, must be taken to heart. Foreign interests too often use "sweetheart deals" with business people and relatives of leadership in order to gain undue influence.[15]

These are just a few examples of *Unrestricted Warfare*, barely scratching the surface of the very comprehensive effort underway. One additional recognition is required, however. While China is clearly active in spending, loaning, and investing money around the world, the Chinese banking system is rapidly adding extraordinary debt. One recent estimate is that the Chinese banking system has rapidly grown to $35 trillion, far greater than their annual GDP.[16] At some point, this also must be viewed as a global systemic risk. Beyond that, China continues to suffer from the second-order demographic consequences of their "one Child policy."[17] China risks serious corruption with consolidated power. China faces the challenge of misallocation of resources that results from central planning rather than market determinations.

In summary:

1. The Chinese are **not** primarily economic investors. They are geostrategic investors. While there are no doubt exceptions, this general truth is a natural consequence of centrally planned economy with geostrategic objectives. In this case, the objective is a hundred-year marathon to displace the United States as the primary superpower (to "de-Americanize the world" and replace it with *The China Dream*).
2. While Chinese foreign investment may be extremely welcome in many parts of the world, it must be made known that such investment arrives with multiple strings. The Chinese expect recipients to adopt their worldview. This is tantamount to conquest by acquisition and investment.
3. All of this must be viewed through the lens of *Unrestricted Warfare*.
4. China faces many challenges. Their use of debt and loans may be or become a serious danger to the global financial structure. They also face challenges at home from demographics and corruption. In order to maintain centralized control, China is increasingly authoritarian, using multiple forms of pressure both on citizens and foreigners.

---

[15] Schweizer, P. (2018). *Secret empires*. New York, NY: HarperLuxe, an imprint of HarperCollinsPublishers.

[16] Theweek.com. (2018). *Chinese banks are big. Too big?* [online] Available at: http://theweek.com/articles/771201/chinese-banks-are-big-big [Accessed 22 May 2018].

[17] Newsweek. (2014). *One-Child Policy Is One Big Problem for China.* [online] Available at: http://www.newsweek.com/2014/01/24/one-child-policy-one-big-problem-china-245118.html [Accessed 22 May 2018].

The essential first step to address these threats is to recognize the fact that what we see as a marketplace, our enemies view as a battle space. We must recognize that a global economic war is already underway with dramatic consequences. We must prepare cogent responses that take into account both national security and economic implications.

Thank you for the opportunity to address this committee and share my concerns and recommendations.

Mr. ROHRABACHER. Well, thank you all for some very fine testimony and we have some questions for you now, and let me just note, Mr. Freeman, that I remember very well Tiananmen Square and, quite frankly, most people don't relate this to the fact that Ronald Reagan brought down the Berlin Wall and Ronald Reagan helped win the Cold War with the Soviet Union.

Tiananmen Square—Ronald Reagan wasn't President, and I have always assumed that had he been President that the democracy movement in China would not have been annihilated in front of us without any type of response that at the same level as the magnitude of what they had just done, and they had just derailed everything that we had always thought, well, China will get better economically and then become more democratic.

But what happened, of course, it became more economically viable and then the powers that be slaughtered those people that would want democracy and, by the way, somebody said, well, what would Ronald Reagan have done—would he send in the troops.

Let me just note I believe Ronald Reagan, when he heard—now, we knew that those troops were massing to come in and attack the people at Tiananmen Square. We knew that. We had the intelligence. Everybody knew that—that we knew it.

Ronald Reagan would have gotten on the phone the day before and said to whoever was the head of the government and say to them—said, you're going to have to back away from sending your troops in and slaughtering the pro-democratic movement in Tiananmen Square—we see you're massing your troops—don't send them in—or no more credit, no more investment—no more American open door to economic interaction between our countries—no more transfer technology. You make your choice, but there will be a big penalty to pay.

Reagan would have done that, and you know what? There wouldn't have been that slaughter at Tiananmen Square. George Herbert Walker Bush was President, and I know when the call that—we all know about what he said in his call. Nothing—he didn't make the call. He knew that was about to happen. He knew there about a slaughter about to happen—a reversal of the democratic process in China but did not—decided not to act.

That, I believe, was one of the most damaging actions or inaction that I have ever seen taken place in my lifetime, because it has left us right where we are at where we have a monstrous now regime in Beijing, and let us note when you're talking about the person who is trying to decide whether to invest in China or Russia that there have been in Russia at least there—opposition parties were forming.

You actually had a people who were starting independent press operations and discussions and there was an opposition and not anywhere near what was acceptable but there was a lot of political reform compared to under the communist era.

In China, there has been no political reform. Zero. There are no opposition parties in China and there is no opposition, and if somebody says anything bad about the government they are hunted down and put in jail, and that's the type of regime.

So it is important for us to consider that that is a factor in the decision making we are making for economic activity. We are now dealing with a flawed government.

We are dealing with a government that has never reformed at all.

With that said, I—there is a couple points that were made here that I would like to just bring up, and the idea that every investment by China is the equivalent of a sovereign investment fund from other countries where the government is actually sending over investment, the companies—when Chinese companies come in and buy—so I have this for the panel—when a Chinese company comes in to buy something in West, is that Chinese company—is there a chance that the Chinese company actually is owned by the Chinese military, and is there any other example where a military is coming in to another country and buying economic assets?

I will just leave that with the—go right down the line on that.

Mr. LE CORRE. As you know, Mr. Chairman, in the '90s some of the PLA companies started to go civilian and started to get involved in other things, not just military but also infrastructure, hospitality, food business, anything.

There are PLA-related companies investing worldwide. They are not even hiding it. But I would say that the big picture is that most Chinese investments in Europe in particular are made by state-owned companies, whether they are security related or not, and they are directly tied to the Communist Party of China and those are private companies——

Mr. ROHRABACHER. I guess a state-owned company—the difference between a state-owned company and the People's Liberation Army owned companies is that the guy over here doesn't have a uniform on.

Mr. LE CORRE. Right. Yes, you're quite right.

On the other hand, it's the People's Liberation Army, which belongs to the Party—to the Party at the very top, and the state-owned companies are more or less government entities and it's a party state. So, you know, it's pretty much all tied up.

Mr. ROHRABACHER. Mr. Chang.

Mr. CHANG. The important thing is that you do have the state enterprises. They act at the direction of the state and, more important, at the direction of the party.

What is really interesting is Huawei Technologies, which is nominally private. This was started by a colonel in the People's Liberation Army who had recently been mustered out.

It has become within, like, two and a half decades—as I mentioned, the world's largest equipment provider—a telecom equipment provider.

How this occurred and by a private company started from scratch is beyond the—unless we can explain that the People's Liberation Army, in this particular case, and perhaps some elements of the administrative state security were behind Huawei, and certainly we know that China's diplomats have been very aggressive in their helping Huawei get contracts in various countries.

This sort of leads us to a conclusion that sometimes it doesn't really matter whether a company is state owned or whether it's nominally private because the state and the party have objectives and they will try to accomplish those objectives through these commercial enterprises.

You know, they often, as Mr. Le Corre talked about, will do it through state enterprises because they do have more control. But nonetheless, even if a company is private, as Huawei is, it is still very much an instrumentality of the state.

And if I could just take 2 seconds to mention your initial point, China has—you know, people say China is authoritarian these days. It started out, obviously, totalitarian in the 1950s with Mao Zedong.

People have talked about sort of the reform. It's now become a mild authoritarianism. Under Xi Jinping, the current ruler, we are basically going back to totalitarianism, because the technology investments by the Chinese state permitted to do things which Mao never could do—so, for instance, the one example that has popped up in the last couple months is this assigning of a credit score to every individual.

And it's not just credit score as what we have in this country. It is looking at social credit—in other words, people's political opinions, your jaywalking record, all of this is a constantly updated score, which gives the ability to control people.

And we saw that about a month ago when a dissident was not permitted to go on a plane because his social credit score was too low, and we are seeing, of course, the—just the power of the state magnified through technology.

So we can say that this is basically now a totalitarian state or one that will be there very quickly.

Mr. ROHRABACHER. Well, luckily they had some American companies that could come over and computerize their system so they'd be more efficient.

Mr. CHANG. And sold them equipment.

Mr. FREEMAN. I would just add on to what Mr. Chang shared, when you couple the social credit score with the facial recognition technology software that's been developed, the Chinese Government has the ability to pinpoint an individual in a crowd of 100,000 in a matter of seconds, and then you couple that—they know exactly who that person is and they can identify them.

It does lend itself to a totalitarian state. We should keep in mind that there are really two types of capital flows that come from China.

One of them is state controlled—whether it's through the banking system which is government controlled, through the People's Liberation Army's companies—or through state-controlled companies.

And the second type of capital flows, which they are cracking down on—there are some very wealthy people in China who would like to see their money get out.

And so they attempted to do that through noneconomic investments but in this case they're willing to be noneconomic, meaning take a bad deal, if they can get money outside of the China and the Chinese Government has really seriously cracked down on that recently.

For the example of Huawei Technologies, I will throw one more anecdote. I had dinner recently with a former member of the board of Huawei. He is an American. He was at an American company that was sold and purchased by Huawei and as part of the purchase deal he was asked to sit on the board of directors.

He said it was surreal to attend board meetings because he would go to board meeting. He would have someone as translator tell him things were clearly not what the meeting was discussing and they fed him nicely and they took good care of him and they told him absolutely nothing, and there were always two observers from the government watching every activity that took place at the board meeting.

And so in many cases—in every case where there is an investment from the Chinese Government thorough any of the mechanisms we discussed, it is government controlled.

There is no question.

Mr. ROHRABACHER. Mr. Meeks.

Mr. MEEKS. Thank you for your testimony.

And I want to go back now to some of what I guess the title of the hearing, the EU and China trade and investment relations—talk about Europe a little bit, talk about—even given similar lines of questions that we've had—some that I had down here.

Let me just deal with that first. For example, in listening to the testimony you had about China, I think many of the same things can be said about Russia with Mr. Putin or so it looks like he's going to be there forever—same thing like China—looks like authoritarianism has been there in regard to Russia in the direction we are moving in.

And so to a degree I was wondering whether the Kremlin and Beijing, do they align where they are looking particularly in Europe and if not where do they differ where they're looking to move particularly in Europe and if not where do they differ, and do know what their views are on the EU, both the Chinese and the Russian.

Mr. Le Corre.

Mr. LE CORRE. Thank you, Congressman.

I do believe that Russia and China are very different countries. Even though I agree with you there is this authoritarian common denominator perhaps.

One big difference, of course, is that Russia doesn't have money and that China does. In Europe, and particularly in the weaker parts of Europe, if you think about southern Europe or Eastern Europe and even the countries outside of Europe, as Mr. Chairman mentioned, in the Balkans, in particular, there is a real need for cash and for help and technology. I mean, the sort of basic technology that a bridge or have a railway or sometimes an airport——

Mr. MEEKS. With infrastructure.

Mr. LE CORRE. And infrastructure. Then the Chinese are very good at this. Now, Russia is basically being—infiltrating some of the local politics of these countries, as we know, just like it happened here in this part of the world. But it's happening in many Eastern European countries and even in Greece for example.

China is a completely different story. They are not really infiltrating the domestic politics. They are buying some kind of influence by investing, by trading, and by putting together some projects in many of these countries.

If you take, again, the case I was referring to of Portugal and Greece, in Portugal they are basically investing in the oil business, in the electricity business. They have a share in the aircraft carrier TAP. They have the largest insurance company. They have a group of private hospitals. They have invested in the media.

So, indeed, that's—and now there's this project that Congressman Cicilline mentioned which is a possibility of investing in the Azores and President Xi Jinping actually himself visited the Azores and might visit again.

So, talking about EU and a NATO country this is a real concern. And in the case of Greece, we are talking about a hub in the Mediterranean Sea with, of course, it's part of the new Silk Road and China wants to use this harbor as the hub for Chinese goods and link up Greece with Eastern and Central Europe, bring more Chinese companies and putting together new terminals.

So, obviously, that's going to impact the Greek economy very strongly.

Mr. MEEKS. Do you want to say anything, Mr. Chang, Mr. Freeman, on this?

Mr. CHANG. When you talk about geopolitics, Xi Jinping and Vladimir Putin pretty much see the world in the same terms and, clearly, they are coordinating their activities not only in Asia but also in Europe, and we saw that, for instance, during the Syrian civil war.

But when it comes to the economy they are two very different countries. You have China—claims a gross domestic product last year of $12.8 trillion. Probably a little bit less than that, but that's what they claim.

Russia is under $2 trillion and also it's the structure of the two economies that are so different because the Chinese have become the world's largest manufacturer. They do sell products. That's one reason for their Belt and Road Initiative—the Silk Road—and Russia has just basically been selling hydrocarbons.

So when it comes to investment in Europe it's very different. You see the Chinese actually investing in infrastructure, as we just heard, and of course, in technology, which is what I've been focusing in on.

But when it comes to Russia, they have not really been investing. What you see are real estate investments from wealthy Russians, sort of the capital outflow that Kevin was talking about in terms of China. So you see that in Europe. But you don't see the important basic infrastructure, basic technology investments coming out of the Russian——

Mr. MEEKS. Other than maybe in some energy that they're trying to get into, right?

Mr. CHANG. Yes, because that's really——

Mr. MEEKS. That's right. That's what they—so let me just ask this question because I want to go back. And Mr. Freeman, you can jump in on this one or any one.

Because I am concerned about how China is investing and what they're looking to do in some of the policies in Europe.

For example, the so-called Golden Visas, where there's a handful of countries in Europe that have residency permits for sale, allowing wealthy individuals to invest a certain amount of money in exchange for passports. Hungary, for example, their program was the most popular, I think, until sometime last year, and the focus was of interest of DHS and visa waivers program loopholes.

And we found that in Hungary most of the residency permits were given to Chinese investors. So my question is how do these systems work in Europe and what screening process do these investors face, if any at all, and is there any connection between the money invested in Europe and the country's position on issues that's regarding China?

Mr. LE CORRE. If I may, I think each of the countries in Europe has this kind of rule. The entry tickets can be quite different. I think in Malta it's maybe 200,000 euro. You can buy a property or building or an apartment and you can have a kind of resident permit that leads to a passport and indeed and EU passport.

And so, even the U.K. does that and Portugal, again, Greece, Italy. Can I just take this opportunity to say that there is indeed a discussion going on now at the European Parliament about screening foreign investment and I think this is a very timely meeting we are having now because at the moment I looks like members of the European Parliament are drafting a law that will be—that will give a far wider definition of, you know, critical infrastructure and technologies that could trigger the screening process.

In effect, the idea is that any investment that affects national security issues and some critical infrastructure—that's why the definition of infrastructure is so important—will now be discussed.

The problem is when you have 28 nation states, how many of those will actually support that bill. The European Commission will then try to pass this—to implement the text that the European Parliament is working on.

But many countries, because they have golden visa rules—because they have Chinese investments—mainly Chinese—will basically raise their hand and say, we don't want to take part in this—we don't want to offend Chinese investors.

That is the situation now. My own feeling is that we will probably end up with a nonbinding mechanism that will at least create opportunities for debate, which is somewhat lacking in many of these countries which we refer to.

Mr. MEEKS. Anything, Mr. Chang, you want to say——

Mr. CHANG. There's another issue here, which is in addition to the screening rules that are under consideration at the EU, there's also talk of a bilateral investment treaty between the EU and China.

And, of course, when we are talking about curbs on acquisition of technology, that will be one of the more important things that is under consideration.

Now, in the United States, we also have the discussions of a bilateral investment treaty which, at this particular time, is going nowhere.

And I think that that's a good thing, largely, because of some political considerations and also because the Chinese just don't honor their obligations, as the chairman talked about.

So I think that if we would have a bilateral investment treaty, it would really be we'd honor it and the Chinese wouldn't, and I think that's probably the same thing with regard to Europe because the whole issue will be enforcement.

But there is that issue out there and it does affect us because, as I mentioned, Europe is the big hole through which a lot of Western technology goes to China, which they can't get in the United States.

So when the Europeans talk about an investment treaty, we have a direct and vital interest in that.

Mr. FREEMAN. Congressman Meeks, I would like to first address the Russia-China question and then I'll—in the year 2008 I mentioned Russia literally attacked our financial system.

They sold off every holding they had in Fannie Mae and Freddie Mac. They did it in time before the election to influence the election.

They asked the Chinese to join them in 2008 and the Chinese chose not to. They were not prepared for it.

In the year 2013, it became official Chinese policy to de-Americanize the world. Vladimir Putin is in alignment with this policy. It is a policy to create under the auspices of the BRICS nations—Brazil, Russia, India, China, and South Africa—to create alternatives to the Western system and they've created an alternative to our SWIFT trading system, to our development banks, to the World Bank, to the International Monetary Fund.

They're preparing for a time in which China is the primary economic superpower of the world and they've been addressing that.

And on the second question on investments, the mention of literally buying a passport, buying residence and so forth, we have a program similar to that in the United States called EB5, and the Chinese have been extraordinarily active.

And I have a friend who is an EB5 attorney and he says, I question all of the people coming from China—I don't know if they're representing the state or representing themselves.

And I point to an example that just recently happened. The Justice Department got sentencing on a Chinese national individual who came to the United States, attended LSU, got a Ph.D. at LSU and went to work as a model employee in a specialized rice company where they made special rice seeds, that on those rice seeds you could do certain type of experiments for biotechnology and so forth—very valuable rice seeds.

There was a visiting delegation from China that came to tour the plant and to visit with him, and on their way out of the country, Customs tore open their suitcases and found that they had stolen millions of dollars' worth of these rice seeds.

That was an investment of human capital that the Chinese made decades ago by sending a student here that went all the way through, got the Ph.D., and worked for quite some time for this rice company.

And the Chinese—they have two things. They have a very long-term view in their investment process and what they want to achieve, and the second is it's always geostrategic—it is not an investment in order to get traditional returns on the dollar.

Mr. MEEKS. Let me just say, and then I am going to yield.

That's one of the reasons why I was a huge supporter of TPP because it set some rules that we could still set, you know, with our allies, et cetera, that says these would be the trade rules in which we will continue to operate with, and I think that they would put some additional pressure on Russia.

But, unfortunately, we pulled out of TPP. And I just have to ask one other thing. Based upon what I think Mr. Chang said, my curiosity was raised because I think you mentioned China specifically what they were doing in the EU.

What—is anything different when—or how does countries outside of the EU, for example, Turkey or Switzerland, how do they deal with the Chinese and the Chinese investments?

Mr. LE CORRE. The Swiss have been told by the Chinese that they are the final destination of the Belt and Road Initiative. So have many other countries.

I guess they are fairly relaxed about Chinese investments. As you know, the largest ever Chinese foreign investment has taken place in Switzerland.

They bought a huge agribusiness company called Syngenta and the deal was finalized just last year—$46 billion U.S.

So Switzerland, a neutral state in the middle of Europe, is actually also attracting investment. I guess everybody is after new investments.

But, of course, Switzerland has a very special political system, hasn't got a real mechanism, and not being a member of the EU might actually, being a weakness in that particular case, as I was referring to the mechanism that is now being discussed.

Mr. ROHRABACHER. Mr. Chang looks like he really, really wanted to make a point.

Mr. CHANG. Maybe 1 minute, and that is for every large European acquisition there is almost always a U.S. subsidiary which gives the U.S. the right, under our legislation, to review it.

We allowed and cleared the Kuka acquisition. But we didn't clear Aixtron. And, you know, going forward, this is one area where I think the United States can actually use some leverage, because in the case of Aixtron, it was December 2016 that the administration refused to permit that.

It was in October of that year Germany withdrew its approval for the Aixtron acquisition but only because the Obama administration pushed it to withdraw the refusal—the permission.

And so it seems to me that, you know, we've seen under the Trump administration the same attitude toward these types of investments. And so I think this is one area where even without a change of EU legislation the U.S. will have a lot of influence if we choose to use it by working with our European partners so that they themselves withdraw approvals for all sorts of deals.

Mr. CICILLINE. Thank you again to our witnesses.

Your testimony had been very useful in, I think, understanding Chinese economic power and their willingness to advance their national interests by the use of these very powerful economic tools and what kind of challenge that represents to the West including the United States.

You have described it as buying influence and a strategy to work with BRICS countries to really establish an alternate kind of international framework. And I think these—the issues that we are discussing today present very serious and complicated challenges for the West and for the United States and I think the one thing that's particularly important is that we need to have confidence that as we are navigating this challenge is that there are people in important positions making decisions that are decisions that we can have comments or in the best interest of the United States and in the national interest of our own position in the world.

And it's why I just want to start by saying how ironic and disturbing at the same times it is that this hearing is happening at the moment that we just learned about revelations related to the President's actions in China.

And, of course, I am referring to the President's very extraordinary steps as it relates to a Chinese company, ZTE, that was found to conspire to sell American technology to hostile regimes in Iran and North Korea.

The Commerce Department had banned American firms from selling parts or providing services to ZTE. But President Trump inexplicably reversed these restrictions on May 22nd and announced an agreement with Beijing to lift the ban on ZTE in an effort to protect Chinese jobs, which I didn't know was actually an objective of the President.

We then learned just 3 days before this announcement that the South China Morning Post reported that the Chinese Government would be providing $500 million in loans for an Indonesian theme park to be built by a state-owned Chinese company and that that would include several Trump-branded properties—a residential development, shops, a hotel, and golf courses.

So I guess my first question is am I correct in my conclusion that this becomes particularly vexing for the United States if we don't have confidence that those in government are making decisions that are in the best interests of the American people and the national interest of the United States and in fact may be done for the benefit of the Chinese company that provides some financial benefit to a company of the President's. That's just a yes or a no.

Mr. Le Corre.

Mr. LE CORRE. Well, my understanding is that this Congress has been very convinced that the rules should be implemented with regard to what you were referring with ZTE and Huawei, these companies that have breaking the rules by selling technologies to North Korean and Iran, which would just be fair enough when you think about the situation with Iran at the moment, which is another sort of transatlantic rift, so to speak.

I do believe that most of this Congress is in favor of implementing this regulation.

Mr. CICILLINE. I guess by question is does that action by the President undermine our effort to respond to this growing challenge from the economic power of China and their use of it to buy influence and change national policies in the West?

Mr. LE CORRE. I certainly would agree with the fact that Chinese influence around the world had been a lot about money and about throwing money at projects and because it controls a lot of cash really.

The state—the party, they are at the helm of the system that is really allowing them to send these state-owned companies to build projects and that can happen pretty quickly.

And even the private companies—usually receive green lights and receive money from a Chinese fund/bank which is always a stakeholder. There's no such think as a private bank.

So yes, in that respect I would agree with you.

Mr. CHANG. I can't speak to motivation on ZTE but there are two things which I think are important about that for the U.S. Congress.

So, for instance, ZTE is the fourth largest maker of telecom equipment in the world. The first largest that I mentioned is Huawei Technologies.

We sanctioned ZTE last year and we ended up with a plea deal because they were violating Iran and North Korea sanctions.

About 3 weeks ago, if I am correct, the Justice Department opened a criminal investigation against Huawei for violating those same sanctions both with regard to Iran and North Korea.

And so the issue is going to be what we do with regard to ZTE because there hasn't been any final disposition yet with regard to relaxing the sanctions.

What we do or don't do with regard to ZTE will very much affect the way I am sure Huawei approaches Justice Department action against them, and that's going to be critical for us.

Second thing is we are talking now, because of the withdrawal from the Joint Comprehensive Plan of Action—in other words, the Iran Nuclear Deal—we are talking about increased sanctions on Iran.

Secretary of State Pompeo, who was before Congress—the House—today talked about the toughest set of sanctions ever imposed on a country.

Well, ZTE is an Iran sanctions case. And so if they were to, for instance, reverse or relax that 7-year ban on exports of American technology and products to ZTE, which was imposed by the Commerce Department last month—if we were to relax the sanctions on ZTE, what message would that send to Iran?

So those are two things which I am sure Congress is going to look at. And as I mentioned, you know, the President has talked about relaxing sanctions on ZTE. So has Commerce Secretary Wilbur Ross.

But they haven't done anything yet, and I am sure that it's the pressure from Congress and from others that is going to affect the decisions that the Commerce Department ultimately makes.

Mr. CICILLINE. Thank you.

I just want to return, Mr. Le Corre, you made reference to the impact that Chinese purchase of Lajes airbase would have. I wonder if you'd just speak a little bit about what you think the impact of just the increased Chinese presence in the Azores means for U.S.-Portuguese relations and also are there other examples where you think the Chinese investments have had a—have been success-ful in impacting the national policy of the countries they're investing in, particularly in the area of human rights or rule of law.

Mr. LE CORRE. Right. Congressman, what I am worried about mainly is the lack of debate in Portugal about the issue of Chinese investment.

This is a country with a GDP that's less than 2 percent of the EU's GDP. That is now opening the doors to more Chinese investments on the premises that in 2008 there was a financial crisis and that the troika, which is made of the European Commission, the European Central Bank, and the IMF recommended that the Portuguese privatize some of its public assets, which they did, and the deal was 5.5 billion euro.

We are now reaching 9 billion euro of privatization. That's slightly more than was agreed, and I am fairly concerned about what was announced last week, that China Three Gorges—this state-owned electricity company was bidding or the entire EDP—the Electricidad of Portugal, which is the largest national grid company of that country—that would have huge consequences.

That would have consequences not just for Portugal itself but for the European Union and possible for NATO.

As far as U.S.-Portugal relationships, I am not really an expert. My impression is that the areas you mentioned, at the moment, are not open to Chinese investment and that the Chinese proposals are about putting together a kind of scientific maritime center, which has nothing to do with the military and that NATO has no plans to withdraw from their particular premises.

Mr. CHANG. With regard to the island of Terceira where Air Base Number Four, or Lajes, is located, I would be worried about Chinese investment into the port area because that would be a natural extension of the Belt and Road, and that would give them extraordinary influence on that island, which is going through very difficult times.

This is something, though, that the U.S. Congress can do because this is a U.S. Air Force question. The reason why the Chinese are even thinking about getting into Terceira and to Lajes is because the U.S. Air Force is taking that down to what they call a ghost base.

If that base is kept open, then the Chinese don't really have an opening into that island and into the air base. So this is a question of, I think, U.S. Air Force relations with Congress and what Congress can do to, you know, demand that the Air Force not permit the Chinese to take over that air base—10,800 feet of runway.

Mr. CICILLINE. I wish members of the Department of Defense were here to hear you. That's the argument we've been making for the last 5 years.

So thank you.

Mr. ROHRABACHER. I want to thank our witnesses.

Now what we'll have now is some closing remarks from Mr. Meeks and Cicilline, if you'd like closing remarks, no or yes. But whatever.

And then I will have my own closing remarks.

So Mr. Meeks, you are recognized.

Mr. MEEKS. Of course, when you're the chairman you can get the last word. [Laughter.]

No, I just basically want to thank you for your testimony here. I think that it has been very insightful.

I think we've got to think through everything. You know, I am one, to be quite honest with you, that understands that the world and the globe is much smaller today than it was.

Everything—we talk about globalization and global trade and it's very important. I think we've got to make sure that we have rules and to the degree that those rules bring us together.

So therefore it's important, I think, initially to work with our European allies, particularly, because we do have the same values and we come from the same bases. And so that's why I think that the emphasis should be to try to work with them as closely as we possibly can and see if we can come up—I believe in a rules-based system. I believe that, you know, that it's important to have a WTO and enforce those rules.

And so when there's something that's outside of those rules, then we need to make sure that we enforce them and chastise whoever is out and the penalty may be that we don't do as much trade with them.

But I do think that whether it's, you know, I would be hypocritical if I didn't say that when I first came into Congress I was focussed and I thought that we didn't need to do a permanent and normal trade relations with China.

That doesn't mean that it should be something that's, you know, open ended and that where if they do something wrong we don't come back against them because, you know, I think that that helps when we trade.

It helps us. It helps to have a more peaceful world. Likewise, I was an individual who thought that we needed to end Jackson-Vanik with Russia and we needed to make sure that we had—you know, try to have a better relationship with Russia also so that we can trade with them.

But we just don't do it and ignore all—any of the bad things that they're doing and we've got to be extra mindful, though, of what their motives may be, particularly with certain items that could be—infiltrate our national security.

So though we need to make sure that we are trading that does not mean we just put down our guards and say let's trade. We've got to keep those guards up because there are nefarious reasons at times that these countries will trade with us and/or allies because, you know, sometimes they may not be able to penetrate us but they'll try to penetrate, you know, one of our allies and it's the same result.

That is, ultimately, why I believe that the only way that we can resolve this is with our allies in a unified manner and then we can deal with the—that's why I asked the country about Russia and China being together, in that regard. It's different, clearly. The economy is a different thing that they're trying to promote in regards to industry. But it is extremely important that we try to figure out these two. I don't think that an extreme to one side or the other is going to—is going to be successful. But we've got to make sure that we maintain our national security.

Thank you, again.

Mr. ROHRABACHER. And finally, again, thank you very much, each and every one of you, and some parting thoughts.

I mentioned earlier how Herbert Walker Bush had launched us in the wrong direction by his inaction at Tiananmen Square and how that has to be looked at as one of the great, I would say, cowardly acts that has resulted by a U.S. President—that has resulted in creating a worse world.

Let me just note that WTO happened under Bill Clinton, and Bill Clinton actually kind of snuck that through because I remember we—several of us were demanding a human rights element to WTO and in fact we didn't get that.

And in fact what's happened now we've had WTO and that's one of the reasons why I personally—Mr. Meeks and I disagree on approaches to how to solve problems and that's why he's a Democrat and I am a Republican and that's a good thing about our country that we are good friends nevertheless.

But let me just note that it's the WTO that has—when we talk about the emergence of China and Chinese power, we are not talking about the power of Chinese people. We are talking about the Chinese elite dictatorship, this clique that rules China with an iron fist.

That's who we are talking about that has emerged, and WTO is now—under WTO, all these things that we've heard today have happened under that trade organization and that's why some of us are very suspicious of going with multilateral trade agreements rather than bilateral trade agreements where we can then go to China, as the President has done, and feel very forceful in trying to approach the issues as he sees fit.

Let me just say that ZTE, they, I would say, alarm bells that we have just heard going off may well be justified. We will see. But I notice there have been a lot of alarm bells about President Trump that turned out, when all was said and done, we turned out—some of the things he was doing actually came to our benefit and he has a different approach, a different way.

I think it's very possible that this—his—what he's doing with ZTE may be part of a bigger scheme that he's trying to actually accomplish, and I won't be criticizing him until we see if that's the case, because he may want to do more than just have a 1-day headline on something.

Maybe he has something in mind that will take a few months of making a few maneuvers in order to accomplish.

Trump knows how to prioritize his goals and that's—and so right now, of course, there are a lot of other things. Maybe he's made some understandings with help here. Maybe ZTE is what he's giving them to get help with something else that might be very important to us.

So with that said, and let me just note, again, about the WTO and what's happened since we have gotten into WTO and permitted China to be part of the World Trade Organization, we've had this—everything today has been under that auspices.

And so it's permitted, and what we have witnessed here, however, is an unholy alliance between Western capitalists, who have only one value that makes them decide what they're going to do, and that's how much money they're going to put in their pocket.

And we have had this unholy alliance between Western capitalists, whether they're in Europe or the United States, and these people who control with an iron fist the people of China, and that is something that I think that we would hope that we would be on the side of the people of China and not on the side of their oppressors.

And one last note that I wanted to make on that was that—let's see if I've got it written down here for myself—I had really an important point that I wanted to take. It's because your testimony was so inspiring but I may—oh no, the EB6 and EB5 programs. If the EB5 program represents money, wealth, that's coming from China, being taken out of China as not part of the elite scheme but instead as a way for individuals to extract wealth and bring it here, then it's good. It's not a bad thing. If you have people who want to escape in China and they happen to be able to have carved out a couple million dollars for their family and it's—it makes us stronger and it weakens the regime, that's I think when we are trying to talk about that.

However, if it is part of an EB5 program, it's part and parcel of this scheme that you have outlined today, which is basically utilizing all economic deals as in a way of expanding the government's control or the government's influence here and abroad, then that would be a bad thing.

So I think that we have to take a look at that program very closely because it may well represent people who are conducting their own small revolution against the system rather than some manipulation of the system itself of our capitalist system, because these may not be—these people may not be in control—be controlled by the People's Liberation Army or the clique in Beijing.

So with that said, I think we've had a wonderful discussion and I want to thank all of the witnesses. This has been very enlightening and provoked some really good discussion.

And Mr. Meeks, it's always a pleasure being here with you and we've got—I think we are going to do some great things with this committee and thank you all for being here.

And this hearing is adjourned.

[Whereupon, at 3:59 p.m., the subcommittee was adjourned.]

APPENDIX

SUBCOMMITTEE HEARING NOTICE
COMMITTEE ON FOREIGN AFFAIRS
U.S. HOUSE OF REPRESENTATIVES
WASHINGTON, DC 20515-6128

Subcommittee on Europe, Eurasia, and Emerging Threats
Dana Rohrabacher (R-CA), Chairman

May 16, 2018

TO: MEMBERS OF THE COMMITTEE ON FOREIGN AFFAIRS

You are respectfully requested to attend an OPEN hearing of the Committee on Foreign Affairs to be held by the Subcommittee on Europe, Eurasia, and Emerging Threats in Room 2255 of the Rayburn House Office Building (and available live on the Committee website at http://www.ForeignAffairs.house.gov):

DATE: Wednesday, May 23, 2018

TIME: 2:00 p.m.

SUBJECT: Chinese Investment and Influence in Europe

WITNESSES: Mr. Philippe Le Corre
                     Senior Fellow
                     Mossavar-Rahmani Center for Business and Government
                     John F. Kennedy School of Government
                     Harvard University

                     Mr. Gordon Chang
                     Author

                     Mr. Kevin D. Freeman
                     Author

By Direction of the Chairman

COMMITTEE ON FOREIGN AFFAIRS

MINUTES OF SUBCOMMITTEE ON _____*Europe, Eurasia, and Emerging Threats*_____ HEARING

Day___*Wednesday*___ Date___*May 23, 2018*___ Room___*Rayburn 2255*___

Starting Time __*2:30 pm*__ Ending Time __*3:59 pm*__

Recesses | *0* | (___to ___) (___to ___) (___to ___) (___to ___) (___to ___) (___to ___)

Presiding Member(s)

Rep. Rohrabacher.

Check all of the following that apply:

Open Session ☑
Executive (closed) Session ☐
Televised ☐

Electronically Recorded (taped) ☑
Stenographic Record ☑

TITLE OF HEARING:

Chinese Investment and Influence in Europe

SUBCOMMITTEE MEMBERS PRESENT:

Rep. Meeks, Rep. Cicilline, Rep. Curtis

NON-SUBCOMMITTEE MEMBERS PRESENT: *(Mark with an * if they are not members of full committee.)*

N/A

HEARING WITNESSES: Same as meeting notice attached? Yes ☑ No ☐
(If "no", please list below and include title, agency, department, or organization.)

STATEMENTS FOR THE RECORD: *(List any statements submitted for the record.)*

Attached

TIME SCHEDULED TO RECONVENE _________
or
TIME ADJOURNED ___*3:59 pm*___

Subcommittee Staff Associate